stuck

the places we get stuck &
the **God** who sets us free

AN EIGHT-SESSION BIBLE STUDY

jennie allen

Harper*Christian*
Resources

Stuck Study Guide
© 2011, 2024 by Jennie Allen

Published in Grand Rapids, Michigan, by HarperChristian Resources. HarperChristian Resources is a registered trademark of HarperCollins Christian Publishing, Inc.

Requests for information should be sent to customercare@harpercollins.com.

ISBN 978-0-3101-7029-7 (softcover)
ISBN 978-0-3101-7032-7 (ebook)

All Scripture quotations, unless otherwise indicated, are taken from the Holy Bible, New International Version®, NIV®. Copyright © 1973, 1978, 1984, 2011 by Biblica, Inc.® Used by permission. All rights reserved worldwide.

Scripture quotations marked ESV are taken from the ESV® Bible (The Holy Bible, English Standard Version®). Copyright © 2001 by Crossway, a publishing ministry of Good News Publishers. Used by permission. All rights reserved.

Scripture quotations marked NKJV are taken from the New King James Version®. © 1982 by Thomas Nelson. Used by permission. All rights reserved.

Any internet addresses (websites, blogs, etc.) and telephone numbers in this study guide are offered as a resource. They are not intended in any way to be or imply an endorsement by HarperChristian Resources, nor does HarperChristian Resources vouch for the content of these sites and numbers for the life of this study guide.

HarperChristian Resources titles may be purchased in bulk for church, business, fundraising, or ministry use. For information, please e-mail ResourceSpecialist@ChurchSource.com.

Author Photo © Jessica Taylor

First Printing October 2011 / Printed in the United States of America

For we know that our old self was crucified with [Christ] so that the body of sin might be done away with, that we should no longer be slaves to sin—because anyone who has died has been freed from sin.

romans 6:6–7 NIV

contents

acknowledgments

sarah • bekah • jessica • kimsey • stephanie • michelle • kathryn • joneel • stephanie • marie • holly • amy • pam • gayle • karen • christy • jill • schmale • courtney • jenn • trish • kimberly • april • laura • leah • cassie • elizabeth • natalie

Because we have journeyed through stuck places together.

• shelby • We've tasted God together. jana • molly • katie • heather • I love you. rachel • brooke • chelsa • amanda • carla • ali • sally • monica • christi • lauri • lindsey • melissa • debbie • susan • lisa • tracy • steph • lacey • beth • jarv • dickey • robinson • kym • cheryl • millicent • jennifer • cici • emily • shelley • katmaack • julee • jess • kara • tobie • rubey • elise • ashley • katherine • carey • erika • nicole • aimee • tri-delt • girls • christie • rachel • hayley • cici • jen • joanie • shelley • maggie • kim • abby • christina • jenny • vicki • erin • bette • gail • michelle • ann • jackie • carolyn • zac

note from Jennie

Stuck.

This study began for me out of a deep struggle—a stuck place. It would serve better to call it something a tad more dramatic . . . it was a war. The kind of war that happens inside of you, the kind that nobody sees. God versus me and all my junk. It wasn't something I could even put words to at the time. In fact, those close to me were oblivious to the chaos ensuing behind my gathered exterior.

But it was real and raging, and even though I couldn't describe it, I was keenly aware of its presence and was exhausted by it.

I was stuck. I experienced a sense of bondage I could not name and did not know how to escape. The outside of my life was bright and shiny, but inside I was a mess: anxious, lonely, afraid, and looking for significance.

This study exists because I know I am not alone in this. The more I am let into the deep crevasses of people's hearts, the more I am convinced that every one of us is fighting something. Yet we look out from our secret wars and see people who smile peacefully and seem to be all right—and we smile back at them.

I'm done smiling.

God is about doing something on this planet. He is about doing something in me, and as long as I am privately fighting and losing inside, He is not getting a thing done through or in me.

We are going to take an honest look at the war inside, expose it, and deal with it. God will win this fight, but we have to start fighting it His way, on His terms. The cause of our stuckness will vary, but our common humanity assures us we are all inadequate and broken. Thankfully, we don't have to stay that way.

Many of us have known God for a long time—and honestly, we know a lot—but are we living what we believe? For some, this may be your first encounter with Him. Wherever you are, I ask and pray that you be honest. Pretense and pretending have never really been God's thing. Not much tolerance for it. So my prayer is this study will be a safe place to explore God and your own heart. The state of our hearts and what we believe about God are the two most important things about us.

Jennie

instructions and expectations

Get Honest

This is going to get messy, but it will be worth it. We will be dealing with hidden sin. God wants to do something with that. But until we recognize that we are stuck and in need of Him, we will miss what He has for us. If you consider yourself stuck, perhaps you would be willing to consider a way out, even if it is costly. Be honest with yourself and honest with God. He knows all of it already, anyway.

Engage with Your Small Group

Do not attempt to deal with such a large thing as sin without kindred warriors at your side, fighting with you and for you. Pray, speak truth in love, and hold each other's feet to the fire. Be vulnerable, and do not abandon those who are vulnerable with you. Prepare to go to war alongside these women. Keep your group a safe place to wrestle and discover and also a place filled with truth. John describes Christ as being "full of grace and truth" (John 1:14). I pray that this is how your small group will be described.

And you shall know the truth, and the truth shall make you free.

john 8:32 NKJV

Commit to Being Consistent and Present

Every time you gather with your group, you will be building
your view of God and His plan for reconciliation in our lives. This
study will create a circular understanding of God and His plan,
and missing a week will leave a hole in that circle. Every time you
are in your small group, you will be processing God in your life.
Consistency and presence show respect to God and those around
you in this process.

Please be quick to listen and slow to speak. Lean into the Holy Spirit
as you process together. Speak as He leads. This kind of vulnerable,
Spirit-led communication with your group will help lead to unstuck
lives.

Let every person be quick to hear, slow to speak.

james 1:19

Ground Rules for Group Discussion Time

:: *Be concise.* Share your answers to the questions while protecting others' time for sharing. Be thoughtful. Don't be afraid to share with the group, but try not to dominate the conversation.

:: *Keep group members' stories confidential.* Many things your group members share are things they are choosing to share with *you*, not with your husband or other friends. Protect each other by not allowing anything shared in the group to leave the group.

:: *Rely on Scripture for truth.* We are prone to use conventional, worldly wisdom as truth. While there is value in that, this is not the place. If you feel led to respond, please only respond with God's truth and Word, not "advice."

:: *No counseling.* Protect the group by not directing all attention on solving one person's problem. This is the place for confessing and discovery and applying truth together as a group. Your group leader will be able to direct you to more help outside the group time if you need it. Don't be afraid to ask for help.

Study Design

In the first meeting, your groups' study guides will be passed out, and you will work through the Introduction lesson together. After that, each lesson in the study guide is meant to be completed on your own during the week before coming to the group meeting. Each week begins with a short intro before moving into the portion marked Study. The study portion is followed by four application projects, then closing thoughts from me. The study portion and projects can be completed in one sitting or broken up into smaller parts throughout the week depending on your needs.

These lessons may feel very different from studies you have done in the past. They are very interactive. The beginning of each lesson will involve you, your Bible, and a pen. Work through the Scripture, and listen to God's voice. Hear from Him. Each lesson will conclude with four projects that will allow God to further change your heart and life, and a final word from me. Don't feel that each lesson has to be finished in one sitting; take a few blocks of time throughout the week if you need to.

The goal of this study is to dig deep into Scripture and uncover how it applies to your life, *to deeply engage the mind and the heart*. Projects, stories, and Bible study all play a role in it. You may be drawing or journaling or interacting with the homeless. At each group meeting you will discuss your experience in working through that week's lesson.

What *Stuck* Is Not

We all are products of messed-up environments. Even with the best parents, spouses, and friends, we still have wounds from relationships. The hurt from these relationships takes work to process, and there are many great resources your group leader can suggest that take you deeper into the wounds from your past. I believe in the wisdom of Christian counseling, and there is a time and place for it. Christian counseling is a process I went through earlier in my life, and it truly brought so much freedom.

However, in *Stuck* the focus is intended to remain on God and His plan for us in eternity, and is not intended to be counseling. I believe growing in our perspective of who He is and what He has for us changes the way we view our past hurts and current struggles.

He heals the brokenhearted and binds up their wounds.

psalm 147:3 NKJV

Nothing is more powerful than God getting bigger in our lives. He has the power to heal with a word. My goal as you walk through *Stuck* is that God would get bigger for you and as He does, you would see a new way to do life, led by His Spirit.

introduction: stuck :: 1

Pages 14–18 are intended for you to get acclimated to this study on your own, after you watch the first video.

Flip to page 19 for Video Teaching.

My third child, Caroline, resembles a Norman Rockwell-esque little girl, with her sweet, blue eyes and bob of blonde hair tied in a white bow. She is usually shy and quiet and joyful. One summer weekend we were out at the lake with another family, and obedient Caroline calmly observed the other children as they played wildly all day. She sat and ate her lunch quietly and sweetly, smiling up at us when we asked her if she was having fun.

Later in the day, some geese came over to where she was playing. They were loud and intruding on her little space. So she turned around in front of the family that had admired her sweet disposition all day and screamed at the top of her lungs, "SHUT UP, YOU DUMB GEESE!"

We all have our issues. Most of us just wear a cute bob or smile to cover them up. We're never as sweet as we appear.

I've found it almost impossible to smoosh what I know and believe about God into the invisible dark spaces in my soul. For instance, I know I must forgive. But when my husband misunderstands me or my kids frustrate me and I find myself spinning with anger, how do I apply forgiveness in that moment? As you begin this study, I pray that you will find in God's Word what I found: a chance for God to change me as I see more of Him.

There is a tension that we feel. Most of us know we are stuck and imperfect, broken. But focusing on the reality of our brokenness usually brings about one of two disconcerting responses: we either run to the dark place of rebellion or to the seemingly safe place of covering it up. Shame follows us to both places.

But to admit our stuck places, our sin, propels us out of shame and toward our need for Christ. Both rebellion and self-righteousness are simply attempts to cover reality. We don't measure up. We are a mess. We are imperfect. But to freely state the facts:

I feel jealous. I feel insecure. I feel prideful and judgmental. I don't live like I need God. I feel rage when my kids wake me up in the middle of the night or when my husband comes home late from work. I worry all the time.

To be known and accepted are the two most fundamental needs a human has. But we often sacrifice truly being known for covering the stuff that makes us seem weak or unlovable.

How can we be sure we will survive something so vulnerable as freely revealing our sin?

He who conceals his sins does not prosper, but whoever confesses and renounces them finds mercy.

proverbs 28:13 NIV

There is another place to turn with our sin—a place that is mysterious and invisible. In this place is the One who offers the mercy we need. It fights against our nature to turn to this place, because it pains us to be dependent.

This place is Christ. Christ saved me from my sin eternally . . . but could He daily save me from it, too?

The plan was that He would die. The Son of God would die, paying for the sins of the world. And then in the greatest miracle in history, Christ would be resurrected to life forever, defeating death and giving us the most beautiful hope. Anyone who put their faith in Him would be forgiven. Their sin would be paid for and thrown as far as the east is from the west. It would be a final act making us forever right with our perfect God.

And for those who have put their hope in Christ, that is our reality. However, sin has not left me. I believe in Christ and know that my sin has been forgiven, but I also stand here holding arms full of it. I know I have been made right for eternity. But what about today? What about my short time left on this planet?

How can the gospel bleed into my struggle with fear, with jealousy, with anger?

To paraphrase my favorite quote from pastor and author A. W. Tozer, "As God is exalted to the right place in our lives, a thousand problems are solved all at once."

This is not really a study about our struggles . . . this is a study about God. As we understand Him and His plans and His heaven and His Son's love for us and His grace and on and on . . . a thousand problems are solved all at once. The day after you finish this study, you will still see sin in your life. We will fight sin until we're in heaven, but my hope is your perspective will radically shift, and as God is lifted in your life, a thousand problems will get smaller.

Let me warn you: I will sound ridiculously redundant because I have no other answers for you but God the Father, Christ, the Holy Spirit, and heaven. May They creatively weave Their way into every answer for every problem you face.

It begins with admitting we need Him. We're broken. The story of the entire Bible is our loving, just God calling a sinful mess of a people to need Him. From Adam and Eve to Israel to the church, the message is the same: *You are broken. Come back to Me.* In our brokenness we find our God.

So we begin here in the most vulnerable but freeing spot . . .

We are broken.

single • angry • jealous • insecure • lonely • unavailable • responsible • exhausted • body image • sex • work • house • kids • school • distant • facebook • blogs • adoption • discontent • sad • confused • searching • overwhelmed • the past • grief • shopping • food • money • bitter •

Let's begin by identifying three places that you feel most stuck. List them here:

addiction • friendships • family • numb • disappointed • bored • withdrawn • anxious • prideful • afraid • indifferent • worried • partying • selfish • unmotivated • impatient • broken relationship • hurt • waiting • distracted • conflict • depressed • toddlers • busy • apathetic • denial • unsure

This is a starting place, a chance to put words to some of the places you may be feeling stuck. God has a plan for these spaces, but that plan begins with us recognizing that we need Him, that we need help.

see ::

Watch video session 1: INTRODUCTION: STUCK

Use streaming instructions on inside cover or DVD.

Take notes if you like.

ask ::

Use session 1: STUCK

Conversation Cards for group discussion.

broken :: 2

Work through pages 28–43 on your own before your next group meeting and before you watch the next video teaching.

Universe Problems

I looked around my living room into the eyes of twelve young women. Twelve successful, beautiful women who previously had not felt very safe or comfortable in church or Bible study. They were the kind of sinners who were looked down upon by the "good sinners" (sinners who had better-hidden or more socially acceptable sin) and they knew it or felt it enough to stay away. They lived fast, and yet here they were, hungry for God—hungrier than most "good sinners" I knew. They desperately wanted God, and His offer of unconditional love and forgiveness felt dangerously comforting. For the past few weeks we had studied together, they had been just relaxing into that . . . relaxing into grace. As time passed they were feeling a little convicted about sleeping around and partying. Not much about their visible lives was changing, though all of their invisible lives were.

The last thing I wanted to do was get legalistic with these girls, so I prayed, "God, how do I address sin without taking away from Your grace?"

He led me to Romans 8.

This chapter describes two ways to live. One way is to know God, to be His, to be filled with His Spirit and to enjoy life and peace. The other way is to be enslaved to our flesh, constantly pleasing it, and ultimately feeling sin and death in it all . . . the waste. As I read these verses, I knew these girls in my living room weren't the only ones who needed help. I needed to be broken over my sin, perhaps more than they did. Their eyes drank in every word, and as I watched them long for God, I found myself more worried about my hidden sins than their blatant ones.

See, they knew they needed God. Did I?

We categorize our sin in a grand gesture to feel better about ourselves, better about our lives, when God couldn't care less what particular sin we love. He wants us to see we sin. He wants us to see we are all helpless without Him. And He wants us to sit with hungry eyes, drinking in His grace. But most of us think that we have enough God. We've heard it already . . . heaven and Jesus and forever. We spend more time scrutinizing truth than living it. We get numb and bored. We forget that it is all real. It is all real.

See, when we step into faith with Him, God shatters everything, not just our Saturday night plans. He changes every relationship, how we spend our time, our motives, our passions, how we live and how we die. He strips us of performing and pretending and lays us bare, fully aware of our need for Him. While it is costly and even threatening, it is what we were designed for.

study ::

read romans 8:1-17

study

In the space below, describe the two sides of
the war from Romans 8:1–17. Describe the war:
the characteristics of those who follow the
Spirit of God versus those who live according to
their flesh.

led by the Spirit

_____

_____

_____

_____

_____

_____

_____

_____

led by the flesh

_____

_____

_____

_____

_____

_____

_____

_____

The struggle between the Spirit of God and evil has been warring since before God spun the planets. This is the universal problem: the Spirit of life and peace versus the law of sin and death.

Romans 8:8 says, "Those who are in the flesh cannot please God." It is impossible to please God without the Spirit of God Himself being present in us and without the blood of Christ erasing our sin.

Two drums are beating. We are each born with the drum of our flesh that beats steadily and selfishly, begging for us to meet its every desire. The sound of this drum beats, telling me to get what I need, build my comfortable life, make a name for myself. It is a drum that beats until we die, unless we are given a different drum, a new drum giving life and peace. The new drum has a purpose and overcomes the selfish drum of our flesh. It beats with God's heart. The new drum can overcome the old one, but the old drum must die.

All we like sheep have gone astray; we have turned—every one—to his own way; and the LORD has laid on [Christ] the iniquity of us all.

isaiah 53:6

I was designed to come to the end of myself again and again and again and again, to slip down the rungs of my ladder, until maybe, after years of reaching the end of me, I would consider that I had a problem . . . that I might need something . . . that I might be stuck.

I might need help.

I might need God.

This feeling is not a Christian problem or a pagan problem, a young or an old problem, a rich or a poor problem, or a married or a single problem. It is a human problem. People feel stuck.

Measuring Sticks

God in His goodness supplied our universal need for a Savior. Before time began He knew people would rebel and run from Him, and He made a way to get them back in Christ. In Christ's death I found grace. Grace to be a sinner. Grace to not measure up. Grace for people around me to disappoint me. Grace for my kids and my husband to be human.

It is important we understand the reason why we can be imperfect. We don't have to try to measure up or pretend because God rescued us from that impossible pursuit through the blood of Christ.

Those of us who have been rescued by God have nothing to prove. We can call sin what it is because our sin has been paid for, cared for. We rest in who we are and what God has accomplished for us.

We can even boast in our weakness, because our weakness shows our need for God even more. Grace frees me from having to measure up to the impossible standard, while at the same time, grace motivates me to run from sin and obey God.

Not long ago I gave a talk in which I shared about some struggles I was having with fear and disobedience. A woman approached me afterward and said, "It must be difficult to share all of this." I thought for a moment and shook my head and said, "I am so aware I am no good apart from my God that it actually comes out pretty painlessly. I am forgiven. I don't feel ashamed of the places I need God."

Shame has paralyzed us. We are afraid to come out of hiding and admit we are flawed. It is ridiculous because we are all flawed. God knows it and we know it. Why are we pretending?

If we trust in Christ, we are forgiven.

The space in which we are stuck, lacking, sinful, broken, and in need, is the space in us that longs for God, longs for forgiveness. When we soberly view ourselves and our sin, we see our need and call out for God.

Toward the scorners he is scornful, but to the humble he gives favor.

proverbs 3:34

Once we have tasted that grace, we are compelled to give our lives away because of it. Because God was that good to love us despite our sin. He was that merciful to give everything to make us right with Him. Knowing that kind of grace changes everything. And we long to follow a God like that. A God who is offering life and peace to those who obey Him, to those who follow Him. He is even offering the means to obey and live a life for Him, through the Holy Spirit.

Obedience turns into a response to the love of our God rather than a duty to perform for Him.

We move from focusing on our need to fixing our eyes on the face of God. He changes everything. Andrew Murray, a great pastor and missionary in the nineteenth century, talks about this in his book *Humility.* He defines *humility* as being "fully occupied with God." We must move our eyes from our sin to God or we will stay stuck in our sin. His grace is why we can confess our sin and find freedom. We live in His grace and then we give His grace to everyone we encounter.

"Therefore I tell you, her sins, which are many, are forgiven—for she loved much. But he who is forgiven little, loves little."

luke 7:47

The more we experience forgiveness, the more we forgive.

who are you, Lord? & what do you want from me?

Read 2 Corinthians 12:7–10. In light of what you read, answer the questions above.

discover

I

Where do you go to find life, to find God?

What are the things that steal joy from you?

Identify some of the sources of life and peace and the sources of sin and death for you:

	sources of life and peace	sources of sin and death
In your relationships:	_____	_____
In your home:	_____	_____
In your mind:	_____	_____
In your schedule:	_____	_____
In your daily decisions:	_____	_____

I see another law at work . . . waging war against the law of my mind and making me a prisoner of the law of sin at work within.

romans 7:23 NIV

measure

In the space below, color in the percentage of your life that you live confidently and perhaps independently of God. Then list the areas in which you feel successful and capable, and the areas you feel insecure or weak.

0%	100%

areas I feel successful

_____

_____

_____

areas I am insecure

_____

_____

_____

As we admit our weak places, our hurts, our sin, God can freely move into those spaces. We depend on Him more and on ourselves less as we soberly view ourselves as broken.

For the sake of Christ, then, I am content with weaknesses, insults, hardships, persecutions, and calamities. For when I am weak, then I am strong.

2 corinthians 12:10

How could this verse transform your view of your weaknesses?

project :: 2

imagine

Romans 8 describes the bondage of the flesh and the freedom and life found in the Spirit. As you consider the ways you live without God, either through inner or outward struggles, draw a picture of yourself stuck and a picture of yourself free because of the Spirit. You can use symbols that represent those two conditions, or stick figures.

me stuck

God in me

3 :: project

respond

God lives in me . . . . true or false?

Defend your answer in fewer than one hundred words. Wrestle this out—do not move forward unless the answer to this is clear to you. The implications of this answer are eternal and life-altering. God inside of you changes everything. Is He there?

Work out your salvation with fear and trembling, for it is God who works in you to will and to act according to his good purpose.

philippians 2:12–13 NIV

The Lord says: "These people come near to me with their mouth and honor me with their lips, but their hearts are far from me. Their worship of me is made up only of rules taught by men."

isaiah 29:13 NIV

Faith Questions

Unapologetically I want you to question your faith. Be sure that what you say you believe, you actually believe. I fear we find ourselves in a world of pretending. People are saying they believe, but if they are really honest, God is not in them. They are not even sure He is real.

> *What comes into our minds when we think about God is the most important thing about us.*
>
> ## a. w. tozer, *The Knowledge of the Holy*

Rarely has anyone questioned my salvation. But I think questioning my salvation is the most powerful and loving thing someone can do for me.

Do you understand that no act on your part will achieve salvation for you?

Do you believe that Jesus Christ is the Son of the living God and that He is God?

Do you believe that He took your place in His death on a cross to pay for your sin?

Do you believe that He has risen from death and now sits at the right hand of God the Father?

Have you placed your life in the hands of this God for salvation and hope?

Honestly, all of that sounds a little crazy, but it is pretty simple. I don't think it is a stretch to say we should scrutinize our faith. This is not a box we check on our voting registration . . . this is eternity. We should be 100 percent sure our hope is in Him alone.

I really like our God. He is so different from any human or god I would ever construct. Despite His power and fame, He loved me in my sin and saved me from it. Now I am free—completely, undeservingly free, forever. I would have been happy being a slave for a God, but He adopted me and made me His kid. So many of us have taken God's love for granted. May His love shatter our sin and drive our lives.

see ::

Watch video session two: BROKEN

Use streaming instructions on inside cover or DVD.

Take notes if you like.

notes

ask ::

Use session two: BROKEN

Conversation Cards for group discussion.

notes

mad :: 3

Work through pages 50–66 on your own before your next group meeting and before you watch the next video teaching.

Not Fair

It was an insanely busy week, and piles of laundry were building in every room. My husband, Zac, noticed my laundry shortcomings when his sock and boxer drawer came up empty, and kindly asked if I could please do some laundry. While Zac helps plenty around the house, laundry is my job.

I forget I get mad . . . until I get mad. Approaching this study, I thought I struggled with every stuck place except anger. God saw my pride as a beautiful opportunity to expose the holes in my view of myself and Him.

Because of everything else on my plate, I ignored Zac's kind requests. Due to his lack of clothing, he kept asking, and his requests eventually transitioned from kind to irritated. Eventually, against all human reason, the laundry escalated to a third world war. Laundry somehow turned into so much misunderstanding and hurt. And despite my self-proclaimed good record, I got MAD! I slammed the door and headed out to my favorite coffee shop to work. Sitting with my latte, I pulled out the lesson I was preparing to teach, and guess what the topic was?

MAD.

I couldn't escape. I was face-to-face with the anger I pretend I never feel. I was broken and humbled. Then God convicted me, *Jennie, do I have your attention? Now let's take care of some business.* I still haven't recovered from all that transpired in my coffee-shop encounter with God.

***

One of my dear friends, Elizabeth, came from an exceptionally broken and destructive family—a family whose experience included prison, abuse, and suicide. At sixteen years old, Elizabeth cried in anger to her mentor, "This is not fair! I don't deserve this family, this life!"

Most of us would agree with this outcry from a sweet teenage girl subjected to such a life. But Elizabeth's mentor knew Jesus, and knowing Jesus deeply impacted her response to Elizabeth. She wisely and shockingly replied, "You're right. You don't deserve this life. You deserve hell and death, and so do I. But God's gracious love for us provided a Savior who took our sins and died for them. He didn't deserve death, and we don't deserve life. It is God's grace that we have life at all."

And with that simple word God moved Elizabeth's perspective from disappointment to hope. Her view of her life shifted from anger to gratitude. Elizabeth found freedom from the bitterness that was beginning to mark her life. Today, Elizabeth is one of the most joyful and encouraging people I know.

Our perspectives must shift for us to find freedom. The way we view our lives must shift. The way we view people must shift. We must allow people to fail us, because they are, like us, sinners. To know God, to truly see God, radically shifts our perspective.

As God is exalted to the right place in our lives, a thousand problems are solved all at once. And while it is that simple, it is not easy. The way to freedom is costly. It wrecks us in the best possible way.

I pray that God would mess you up as much as He messed me up that day over coffee and His Word.

study ::

read james 1:19–27

In this passage, what does God tell us about . . .

our response to anger?

_____

_____

our response to the Word of God?

_____

_____

how we live out our faith?

_____

_____

Describe how these verses should affect your life personally.

Describe how living this way could affect those around you.

The most crucial question: do you love God?

If your answer is yes, then there is potential for self-control and love to come from your life—a transformational, unselfish, disciplined love, defusing volatile situations and restoring those who are suffering. This love is the call on every person who claims to know Jesus. This love is so contrary to the world that it has the power to demonstrate God, to put Him and His radical love for His people on display.

This love costs us something. It is not easy, but it is simple.

_____

Bless those who curse you, pray for those who abuse you. To one who strikes you on the cheek, offer the other also, and from one who takes away your cloak do not withhold your tunic either. Give to everyone who begs from you, and from one who takes away your goods do not demand them back.

luke 6:28–30

_____

Anger is our reaction when we feel our rights are being taken from us. We get angry about not getting what we think we deserve. We get angry when our "rights" feel threatened.

But God is calling us to die to these rights.

This is the part that is radical and possibly insane. We are to love those who hate us. We are to be giving to those who don't appreciate it. And in asking us to do this, God is asking us,

Do you trust Me?

Do you trust Me when I ask you to step out on a limb?

Do you trust Me when what I am asking costs you something?

Do you trust Me when obeying Me is excruciating?

Name some of the rights you hold dear:

(ex: a right to pursue happiness, a right to have healthy kids, a right to make a fair salary, etc.)

_____

_____

_____

_____

_____

_____

_____

_____

_____

One of mine is that I feel I have a "right" to be understood. So when my husband is frustrated about laundry and not understanding how much I have on my plate, I feel misunderstood, and therefore I believe I have a right to get mad. I get mad when the line at the grocery store is too long and they don't open more lanes, because I believe I have a right to move quickly through life. I get angry when someone gossips about me, because I believe I have a right to a good reputation.

But then I read something like this . . .

who are you, Lord? & what do you want from me?

Read Galatians 2:20. In light of what you read, answer the questions above.

study

Little Crosses

God is calling us to surrender—a surrender that is so resolute, so final, that to lift our heads in defense or protest would seem ridiculous.

Why would anyone live this way?

An incredible mercy flows out of God, and with it comes an expectation that mercy births more mercy . . . love births more love. When Jesus calls us to be kind to our enemies, He says in Luke 6:35 that even God Most High is kind to the ungrateful and the evil. (*Ungrateful and evil.* He is talking about us without Him there.) And then He says, *You do the same, so that the world will see your love and glorify Me in heaven.*

I (an ungrateful and evil person) receive God's mercy, because Christ laid down His rights in heaven. He is God. He chose to be misunderstood by the world to the point of being brutally killed. And note: He is still God.

He is saying, *You know Me; you do the same. I'll help you and fill you. I will show you when and where to lay down your rights. But let's start with your life, your expectations, your money, your family's approval, your right to a family, your right to move quickly, your right to be successful. I know I am asking a lot. But if you die to all of this . . . I will do things greater than you ever hoped, dreamed, or imagined. But you have to let go. You have to lay down the very things that are most valuable to you, if you love Me. Do you trust Me?*

The problem with anger is really what we believe about God. Do we believe He is worthy of our trust? Do we trust Him to defend us if we stop defending ourselves? Do we believe He knew exactly what He was saying when He said, "Turn the other cheek" and "Die to your rights"?

Or are we too afraid of becoming a door mat?

Jesus wants our dignity to come from Him, not how we are treated.* Christ willingly laid down His life, and nothing was taken from Him that He did not willingly give, even His life on the cross. *Turn your cheek. Give your tunic. Bless. Pray.* The verbs surrounding these difficult commands are active, not passive verbs. There is strength and intention in humility. Whatever attack or injustice I might perceive, however slow the grocery lines or however false some outrageous slander, letting it wash over me without a fight, looking past my offender and at my God, is radical but the most powerful path to freedom.

Freedom is found in:

:: allowing God to defend me, even if that means I don't see it until heaven;

:: accepting that life is not right and fair now, but it will be;

:: loving instead of defending or fearing or fighting;

:: giving freely and not having a sense of entitlement;

:: embracing my faults, rather than proving my point;

:: releasing others' perceptions and understandings of me, and holding on to God's, since He knows my heart;

:: embracing the death of my rights and desires, and receiving His will for me.

He wants us to hear this and trust it, and we don't always know why. He never said it would be easy to follow Him.

Then Jesus told his disciples, "If anyone would come after me, let him deny himself and take up his cross and follow me. For whoever would save his life will lose it, but whoever loses his life for my sake will find it. For what will it profit a man if he gains the whole world and forfeits his soul? Or what shall a man give in return for his soul?"

matthew 16:24–26

We have no literal crosses; our crosses are our rights. Every one of our rights is a little cross that He calls us to die on over and over and over again. Why would I choose to die? Because life is not about me, because this world is not my home, because I'm tired of defending myself, and because the God of the universe is my Defender.

And somehow, even though it feels like death, in laying down my rights I find freedom.

*If you are being physically, sexually, verbally, or otherwise abused, please seek help and safety immediately. God does not call us to live in an abusive situation.

compare

right *[noun]*: a claim you are due or entitled to

Compare the rights you have as human being in this culture to the rights you have as a Christ-follower.

I have been crucified with Christ. It is no longer I who live, but Christ who lives in me. And the life I now live in the flesh I live by faith in the Son of God, who loved me and gave himself for me.

galatians 2:20

---

rights as a human being
(ex: house, independence)

rights as a Christ-follower

list

List some of the things (big or small) that make you angry. Then refer to James 1:19–27 and list God's instructions for us concerning our anger and living rightly.

things that make me angry
(ex: when my kids talk back)

God's plan for my anger
(ex: be slow and meek as I instruct)

_____

_____

_____

_____

_____

_____

_____

_____

_____

_____

_____

_____

Looking at the anger triggers in your life and the commands from Scripture on how to handle them, do you believe that it is really possible to control your anger? How?

imagine

Is there a time that you distinctly remember anger being present in your household during your childhood? Draw a picture of how you felt during this experience.

respond

Do you have unresolved anger in your life?

Yes or No (circle one)

Do you have any quiet anger in your life toward someone? Quiet anger is a small grudge or harbored bitterness toward someone who has hurt or disappointed you.

Yes or No (circle one)

If your honest answer to the last question was yes, what are your plans for moving toward healing and reconciliation?

Describe what it would look like to allow God to work through you instead of reacting in anger when presented with a trigger.

Do not let the sun go down while you are still angry, and do not give the devil a foothold.

ephesians 4:26–27 NIV

Always Exceptions

Is there ever a time for anger?

Of course. Unfortunately, the world is full of injustice. Abuse and neglect warrant our anger. God is angry with sin. We have a righteous anger within us that cries out against injustice, and there are specific times when we need to stand up and defend. The Holy Spirit leads us in how to respond to injustice, big and small, as we lean into Him. There is a time and place for action against injustice and a time and place to pursue reconciliation.

Jesus Christ was misrepresented, mocked, betrayed, beaten, and murdered unjustly while on this planet, and yet He rarely displayed anger. The times He responded outwardly with anger were in situations where His Father was being dishonored (see Mark 11:15–17) or when He was face-to-face with the results of sin, unbelief, and death (for example, John 11:37–38).

God doesn't tell us never to get angry. God's call is that we be slow to anger because He knows we are so easily offended. And in doing this we live like God: "The Lord, a God merciful and gracious, slow to anger, and abounding in steadfast love and faithfulness" (Exodus 34:6).

If Christ, laying down His rights, justified so few reasons on this planet to respond with anger, how many can we justify?

Let's pick our fights wisely.

see ::

Watch video session three: MAD

Use streaming instructions on inside cover or DVD.

Take notes if you like.

ask ::

Use session three: MAD

Conversation Cards for group discussion.

discontent :: 4

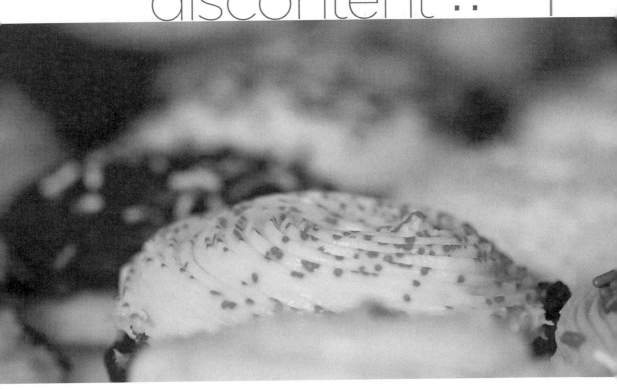

Work through pages 74–87 on your own before your next group meeting and before you watch the next video teaching.

Soul Sick

Right before I turned sixteen, I wanted to be considerably cooler than I had been up until that point. I had a late birthday for my grade. Nearly all of my friends had already turned sixteen and gotten their first car, mostly Honda Accords, small SUVs, a few Jeeps, and one convertible. I longed for my turn.

My turn came. I'll never forget it, when on a warm evening in the spring, my parents came in and said, "Grandmom and Granddad are here, and they have a surprise for you." Dad had a tense smile, gritting his teeth in the way he does when he feels stressed.

Grandmom was holding a set of keys. My heart leaped! They had bought me a car?!

Walking closely with me, they opened the front door to their own car and said, "Surprise! We're giving you our car!"

My new car was a metallic gold 1980s Lincoln Continental that was too big to fit in our garage, sporting a digital dashboard, gold leather interior, and oval windows in the back with gold stars painted in the middle. When you turned on the headlights, two metal garage-door-looking covers folded back.

My only hope at this point was that Mom and Dad would never make me drive this car.

But they did. What was supposed to represent freedom and make me cooler became the source of an obsessive hatred—my nemesis:

the fanciest, ugliest, and largest ride you have ever seen. After hours of pleading, it was clear: I was going to be driving this car. I despised the car so badly, it made my soul sick.

Discontentment is plaguing the souls of women. Our houses are too small; we wear the wrong size; we can't get pregnant; we can't get married; we can't afford the right jeans. We need kids who obey and hair that obeys and husbands who obey, and we need jobs that are fulfilling and enough money to do it all. We need the big things and small things because we want something more, something different. And our souls are sick with it.

study ::

read romans 12:9–21

study

In one column, list all of the commands found in
this passage in Romans; then in the other column
write out the opposite reaction to the command.

with God

(ex: rejoice with those who rejoice)

(ex: let love be genuine)

without God

(ex: envy those who are rejoicing)

(ex: insincere flattery)

_____

_____

_____

_____

_____

_____

_____

_____

_____

_____

_____

_____

_____

_____

_____

_____

_____

_____

_____

_____

Throughout Ecclesiastes, Solomon explored every pleasure on this planet and discovered over and over again things like this:

Then I saw that all toil and all skill in work come from a man's envy of his neighbor. This also is vanity and a striving after wind.

ecclesiastes 4:4

We are chasing wind.

When we were knit together, God spent some time knitting parts of us to need Him. We were created to matter, to be known and seen, and once seen, to be loved no matter what.

These desires are innate; God created these spaces in us.

He wanted us to need Him. It's a funny thought, really. Here is the God of the universe, creating spaces in little people. Desiring for us to need Him . . . want Him . . . be incomplete without Him . . . love Him.

But we don't want Him. Rather than chasing a God who built planets, we chase wind.

Wind Chasing

I believe we miss the freedom God promises because we do not live as if His words need to be applied to our lives. We chase everything under the sun, thinking it will bring us comfort or fill us up, and it never does; it never has. Yet we keep chasing the wind, trying to make it fill all the blank space inside.

Let's go back to the beginning: Adam and Eve wanted to matter, so they ate a piece of fruit. Their son Cain wanted to matter so he killed his more successful brother. A group of people in Genesis wanted to matter so much, they built a huge tower. Their goal: to make a name for themselves. *Make a name for ourselves*. It sounds familiar, doesn't it?

Just like Eve, we want to matter and we want to make a name for ourselves. We want to be significant, and we rarely look to an invisible God for that significance. Instead of eating fruit or building towers, we build houses, wardrobes, friend lists on Facebook, ministries, careers, families, and lives trying to matter and longing to be seen.

We already do matter, and we already are seen.

We each have pictures of how our lives are supposed to be, if we build them just right. Later, we are so disappointed when it does not turn out like we planned, when we realize we tried to fill with other stuff the spaces God knit for Himself. We hunger to the point of starving for Him, and yet we still don't turn to Him.

Here is the problem with us: we don't go to war with our invisible, soul-sickening sin. We deal with the big, showy, obvious sin that everyone sees, but the invisible stuff is trickier, sneakier, deadlier. Discontentment in the form of jealousy, comparison, and greed is making us sick. It washes over our minds constantly, and yet we are so accustomed to it, we have become numb—*stuck*. The more this word is tossed about in my head, the angrier I become. I am angry at the devil, at myself, at this world. I am angry that such small and insignificant dreams bind us so tightly that we live disappointed and paralyzed.

All the while, there is a giant story in the background that we can barely make out because we are so distracted. We are missing the point above it all. The story goes on, whether we choose to care about gold Lincolns or eternal gold crowns . . . the story is happening.

The God of the universe adores us, sees us, makes a way for us, calls us, loves us, saves us, and wants to give us a story within His beautiful story.

While we compare and long and wait and ask and save and spend and flaunt and pretend and cry and whine and tear down and puff up and stare and wish and ignore and complain and demand and search and find . . . we miss something . . . we miss the most important thing . . . maybe we miss the only thing.

who are you, Lord? & what do you want from me?

Read John 12:24–26. In light of what you read, answer the questions above.

consider

Two years ago I sat on my bathroom floor in the middle of the night, reading a blog. That night God changed my life. I read about a girl who had left her dreams for her perfect life and chosen instead at age eighteen to move to Uganda and begin adopting Ugandan orphan girls off the street. Currently at the age of twenty-two, she has many adopted daughters and feeds hundreds more near her home.

Read her words and respond by journaling your thoughts.

Thursday, November 29, 2007

Someone asked me the other day, "Really? Is it really as great as you make it sound? I could never do that! Are you really happy?"

For all of you who wonder, this is my response.

You know what I want sometimes? To go to the mall and spend a ridiculous amount of money on a cute new pair of shoes. I want to sit on my kitchen counter chatting with my girlfriends and eat a whole carton of cookie dough ice cream. I want to watch Grey's Anatomy, or any TV for that matter. I want to cuddle with my sweet boyfriend. I want to hop in my cute car, go to the grocery store, and pick up any kind of produce I want. I want to wake up in a house with my loving family, not all by myself. I want to go to Blockbuster and pick out a movie to watch with my little brother and his friends and I want to cook for them at midnight. I want to spend mindless hours with my best friends talking about boys and fashion and school and life. I want to go to the gym. I want my hair to look nice. I want to wear cut off jean shorts. I want to be a normal teenager living in America. I do.

But.

You know what I want more? ALL the time? I want to be spiritually and emotionally filled every day of my life. I want to be loved and cuddled by 100 children and never go a day without laughing. I want to wake up to a rooster, my two Africa dogs, and a splendid view of the Nile river. I want to be challenged endlessly; I want to be learning and growing every minute. I want to be taught by those I teach. I want to share God's love with people who otherwise might not know it. I want to work so hard that I end every day filthy and too tired to move. I want to feel needed, important, used by the Lord. I want to make a difference and I want to follow the calling that God has planted deep in my heart. I want to give my life away, to serve the Lord with each breath, each second. I want to be here. Right here.

Most people get around twenty-five thousand days on this planet. Katie's blog entry wasn't about Africa; it was about obeying the God of the universe with her short time on earth. She gets it. And once we get it . . . life as we know it, these twenty-five thousand days, are never the same.

What do you want out of this life?

What do you think God wants you to want more?

act

Discontentment often leads to jealousy. We so rarely truly celebrate with people. Think of someone you know who has good news in her life—write her a letter or think of a creative way to go all out celebrating with her. Afterward, come back and write here about how it made you feel.

Rejoice with those who rejoice.

romans 12:15

measure

How well do you celebrate others' successes?

1	2	3	4	5	6	7	8	9	10
never									always

How often do you compare yourself to others?

1	2	3	4	5	6	7	8	9	10
never									always

How often are you thinking of the next thing you want?

1	2	3	4	5	6	7	8	9	10
never									always

How often are you grateful?

1	2	3	4	5	6	7	8	9	10
never									always

How quickly do you respond to people in need?

1	2	3	4	5	6	7	8	9	10
never									always

Write about it.

_____

_____

_____

_____

respond

List the things that it would take for you to never be jealous or discontent again. Seriously, go ahead and name them all. This should be kind of fun. Name everything you could ever want or change about yourself or your life. Go.

_____

_____

_____

_____

_____

_____

_____

_____

_____

_____

_____

_____

_____

_____

_____

Are you going to live for this list or let it go? If you live for it, it will invade all of your thoughts, desires, motivations, time, energies. If you let it go, you will experience freedom to celebrate others, being used by God in any way, and a thought life that has space for others and God.

Either way, you commit.

Gold Lincolns or Gold Crowns?

Recently my high school graduating class celebrated our fifteenth reunion. I couldn't make it, but one of my best friends gave me a detailed report over the phone. One of the first people she told me about was a nerdy, quiet but nice, overweight boy from our class. His name is Luke. She said, "You know Luke is really close to the Lord now?"

I was surprised. I asked, "How did he meet God?"

"Seth shared Christ with him in high school."

Seth was a close friend of mine. He played football. He was cool, although I can't remember what car he drove. When my friend told me what Seth got to be part of, my heart was grieved. While I worried about the car I drove for a few hundred days in high school, Seth was building stories that will last forever and ever and ever.

We will all meet God face-to-face before we know it . . . It seems silly to spend another day being sick over gold Lincolns.

I know of no greater simplifier for all of life. Whatever happens is assigned. . . . Are some things, then, out of the control of the Almighty?

Every assignment is measured and controlled for my eternal good. As I accept the given portion other options are canceled. Decisions become much easier, directions clearer, and hence my heart becomes inexpressibly quieter. . . . A quiet heart is content with what God gives.

elisabeth elliot, *Keep a Quiet Heart*

see ::

Watch video session four: DISCONTENT

Use streaming instructions on inside cover or DVD.

Take notes if you like.

ask ::

Use session four: DISCONTENT

Conversation Cards for group discussion.

Work through pages 94–111 on your own before your next group meeting and before you watch the next video teaching.

Sit 'N Spins

Do you remember the Sit 'N Spin? It was a popular children's toy years ago, and in case you are too young to remember, it was made out of small, round disks with a handle in the middle, and you would wrap your legs around them and sit down and spin yourself in circles. Sit and spin.

That is my brain. My brain is a Sit 'N Spin.

Fear, anxiety, and worry—they plague me. I sit and I spin.

A few years ago my husband felt God's calling to start a church. Starting a church from scratch isn't easy. And in the beginning it feels as if it all is riding on you. Do people trust you, like you, believe in you? You find yourself under an intense microscope. Because I'm a person prone to the addiction of winning everyone's approval, this scrutiny about did me in.

Every morning at 3 a.m. I would wake up and sleepily crawl onto my imaginary Sit 'N Spin and begin hours of worry about the church, people, and our kids' futures. Most of my spinning centered around worrying if we were measuring up to everyone . . . even to God.

We worry about the things we most love. I spin and I worry about the things that matter most to me.

We worry about what we value. I valued the admiration and approval of my family and friends. So I would lie in bed and worry about what they thought. The invisible thoughts of a few people controlled me.

This went on for a couple of years. And more than any other invisible struggle, my struggle with anxiety, fear, and worry birthed this study. Eventually, I had to go to battle with this. It was consuming me, and yet I could not see clearly the answer of how to kill it.

Friends suggested anxiety medicine, counseling, and said things like, "You have to let go!" I was not opposed to these options, but before I did anything else, I wanted to scour the Word of God and see what He wanted for me in this struggle. I just knew that what I believed about God had to impact this struggle. God had to have more for me than medicine and counselors, though I was certain those were tools He could use. I just wanted to be sure before I turned to everything else under the sun, I had first gone completely to Him. *Stuck* is the result of that search.

Months later, as I taught *Stuck* for the first time, I ended up in a group with Heather, a young physical therapist who was pregnant with her first child. Heather had a look in her eyes most of the time that seemed uneasy to me—a look like any minute the bottom may fall out on her life and she was doing her best to prepare mentally.

As we all shared about the invisible places in our souls where we struggled and areas with which we did not trust God, she confided that she lived in fear of having a special-needs child. She actually cried as she shared this very real fear. See, most of Heather's life was spent working with special-needs kids. She was not sheltered with false optimism. She knew this was a possibility for every family having a child, and she feared it so much that it was stealing the joy of giving birth to her firstborn daughter. Fear was holding her captive.

study ::

read matthew 6:25–34

Unlike the lilies, do you feel yourself laboring and spinning? Describe it.

As you read how He cares for living things of far lesser value than you:

What do you believe about God's power to care for you?

What do you believe about His ability to see you?

What do you believe about His affection toward you?

What does He say about how we are to move forward without fear?

(Note: Do not just write, "Seek first the kingdom of God." What does it look like to actually do that in your life?)

With no God, we value only what we see. We value today because it is all we have. But if that other kingdom is real and does last forever, something must change. We have to face what we fear.

He himself bore our sins in his body on the tree, that we might die to sin and live to righteousness. By his wounds you have been healed.

1 peter 2:24

Our freedom cost Christ everything. Because He died and defeated sin and death in His resurrection, we have the power to "die to sin." Freedom did not come cheap, but it is there for us to take freely. Surrender is difficult, but God calls us to it because when we die—die to our hopes for our lives, our need to please everyone, our demands, our fear of failing, our need to promote ourselves, our control, our fear of loss and hardship—we find freedom. He brings life from death . . . God can do that in us.

God is asking us, *Do you trust Me? Do you trust me when your life is out of your control? Do you trust Me when you lose your job? When your husband loses his job? Do you trust Me when your child is rebelling? Do you trust Me when you are being misunderstood? Do you trust Me when you are craving to be married and there is no potential husband in sight? Do you trust Me when I ask you to risk your comfort, your security?*

No one ever told me how insane Christianity was before I signed up.

No one told me that it would cost me everything.

But in surrendering everything, we find freedom.

This is the blessed life—not anxious to see far in front, nor eager to choose the path, but quietly following behind the Shepherd, one step at a time. . . . The Oriental shepherd was always out in front of the sheep. He was down in front. Any attack upon them had to take him into account. Now God is down in front. He is in the tomorrows. It is tomorrow that fills men with dread. God is there already. All the tomorrows of our life have to pass Him before they can get to us.

rev. f. b. meyer, *Streams in the Desert*

The LORD is my shepherd. . . . Even though I walk through the valley of the shadow of death, I will fear no evil, for you are with me; your rod and your staff, they comfort me. . . . Surely goodness and mercy shall follow me all the days of my life, and I shall dwell in the house of the LORD forever.

psalm 23:1, 4, 6

who are you, Lord? & what do you want from me?

Read Isaiah 2:2, 17–18, 22. In light of what you read, answer the questions above.

Little Statues, Big People

We won't be here forever; another kingdom is coming. And when it comes . . . when He comes, He will come expecting us to be waiting for Him. But many of us will be holding things we valued more. Those things we hold and spin over—they are idols. He is jealous for our affection and our trust, and rightly so. He is God, our Creator, our Redeemer. As we worry and spin and pretend there is no God, He watches us. He sees us doubting His provision and plan. And He thinks to Himself . . .

For my thoughts are not your thoughts, neither are your ways my ways. . . . For as the heavens are higher than the earth, so are my ways higher than your ways and my thoughts than your thoughts.

isaiah 55:8–9

As I sat spinning about the invisible thoughts of a few people, God watched with His knowledge of forever. Thankfully He clearly called me to die to something I thought was so big, but He knew was so small. Caring about what others thought had become an idol that I loved more than God. And in His goodness He showed me how much I held on to. How much I loved what they thought more than I loved Him. How much I cared about their opinions rather than His.

I couldn't keep living for both.

If I were still trying to please man, I would not be a servant of Christ.

galatians 1:10

My friend Heather continued to move through the study. She was honest and sought God with her fear. On the last night, as we were leaving our discussion of what God had done, Heather shared something so beautiful, so far from a false hope or pretend faith. Heather said, "I am not afraid of having a special-needs child anymore. In fact, if that is what God has for me, that is what I want for my life. We are only here for a little while, and if He gives me that hard thing to make Himself known, I am okay with that."

Heather had a beautiful, healthy baby girl. But no matter how God had designed her daughter, in facing her fear and running to God with it . . . she died to an idol, the idol of an easy life and a healthy child. She was overturned in her spirit. She was set free.

Sin isn't only doing bad things, it is more fundamentally making good things into ultimate things. Sin is building your life and meaning on anything, even a very good thing, more than on God. Whatever we build our life on will drive us and enslave us. Sin is primarily idolatry.

tim keller, pastor and author of *The Reason for God*

study

Fear and worry hold us back from all that God wants for us. My hope
this week is that you would be overwhelmed by the cause of Christ
for you, so overwhelmed that it would flood you with courage.

measure

How much of your thought life is consumed with fear or insecurity? Draw a percentage on the pie chart. Now list the things that consume your mind the most. What are you worried about?

Take every thought captive to obey Christ.

2 corinthians 10:5

Do you believe you have control over your thought life? How can you do that?

imagine

Imagine God wrote you a personal letter concerning your fear. How would He say your fear limits you? Does He see you? Is He taking care of you and those you love? Does He want you to have freedom from these thoughts and insecurities? Now write that letter, incorporating the scriptures we have studied this week.

answer

Do not be anxious about anything, but in everything by prayer and supplication with thanksgiving let your requests be made known to God. And the peace of God, which surpasses all understanding, will guard your hearts and your minds in Christ Jesus. Finally, brothers, whatever is true, whatever is honorable, whatever is just, whatever is pure, whatever is lovely, whatever is commendable . . . think about these things. What you have learned and received and heard and seen in me—practice these things, and the God of peace will be with you.

philippians 4:5–9

What are we commanded to do with our anxiety?

What guards your heart and mind from fear?

What should replace your fearful thoughts?

Where is peace found?

How well are you living out these truths? Where are you putting your hope?

identity

The verses you are about to read have completely changed the way I approach God. Life is found in death. Read the verses several times, and respond to the questions below.

For we know that our old self was crucified with [Christ] so that the body of sin might be done away with, that we should no longer be slaves to sin—because anyone who has died has been freed from sin.

romans 6:6–7 NIV

Describe how Christ bought your freedom with His death.

Describe how freedom can be found as we die to this life.

How is God specifically calling you to die to this life and to any idols you may have?

How would dying to these things impact your struggles with fear and worry?

Fill in the blank.

_____ must get smaller for God to get bigger in my life.

Bigger Fear

But he is unchangeable, and who can turn him back?
    What he desires, that he does.
For he will complete what he appoints for me,
    and many such things are in his mind.
Therefore I am terrified at his presence;
    when I consider, I am in dread of him.
God has made my heart faint;
    the Almighty has terrified me.

job 23:13–16

I was so anxious, living tied up in knots, but everything shifted for me when my fear of God got bigger than my fear of people. The bigger God gets in my life, the less I live in fear of people and the more I live in fear of God Himself. He is God and is so jealous for us. He doesn't leave us to our seemingly innocent idols. He calls us to lay them down.

I wish this would have been a once-and-for-all death to all my idols. But as Jesus told the men who loved Him, *If you are going to keep following Me . . . you are going to have to deny yourself the things you love on this planet and take up your cross daily and follow Me.*

Daily I have to die to the idols in my life. I die to these things so that I can follow Jesus. I can't hear Him, see Him, or follow Him as long as I love something more than Him. Daily I die to the idols in my life so that daily I can follow Him.

I fall away so easily. Things I can see are quicker to comfort and follow than things I can't see.

But I want to live for the things I can't see, the things that last forever. It is worth it to die every day I am here on earth . . . which isn't that many. Let's go die—die to the things we love more than God today and tomorrow and the day after that.

see ::

Watch video session five: SCARED

Use streaming instructions on inside cover or DVD.

Take notes if you like.

ask ::

Use session five: SCARED

Conversation Cards for group discussion.

overwhelmed :: 6

Work through pages 118–133 on your own before your next group meeting and before you watch the next video teaching.

Big Things

What if God actually has things He wants us to do today?

But we aren't listening.

My oldest children were one and three years old when God made it clear that I was to enroll in seminary alongside my husband. The thought of papers and massive books to read overwhelmed me, to say the least. Several people close to me questioned this calling, for good reason. How could I take on such a large endeavor during the most demanding years of motherhood? I knew if this was not God's will, my family would suffer. But both my husband and I felt confident God was in this.

So I told God, "I will listen to You, if You will speak. I will ask You about how to spend my time. I will respond to Your Spirit even if it does not make sense."

God delivered. When I would open an invitation for a party, be invited to a play date or a trip with friends, even run errands or have days off—before I would respond or do anything, I prayed.

He answered. He led me with His Spirit by giving me peace or an uneasy feeling. By following His lead, I got through those three years with meaningful relationships, a passionate understanding of God from my studies, and intact, beautiful relationships with my husband and kids. Looking back, they were some of the most peaceful years of our lives. We loved it. We grew and we saw God move.

He was so real to me when I needed Him and leaned on Him. He showed me that He actually has plans for my days here. I trusted that God had a plan for my life, and He proved faithful.

One of my best friends, Kathryn, tried a similar experiment during a tumultuous time in her life. After trying unsuccessfully to control her overwhelming life, she prayed, "Okay, God. I am going to swing the pendulum the other way here, and I am going to trust You to lead me."

She decided to sit still and listen to God's voice before trying to interfere and fix her situation. She also told God that she would say no to every single thing that came her way unless she was convinced it was from Him. She wanted to let Him control not only the big, difficult situations but also the smaller details of her life and schedule. Kathryn handed Him everything . . . she was willing to do anything. As she said no to more, God opened opportunities that were designed for her, opportunities that brought Him so much glory and brought her so much joy.

study ::

read ephesians 2:1–10

In Ephesians 2, there are two spirits to follow.

What are the characteristics of people who follow the ways of the world?

What changed when Christ rescued people from that rule?

For what purpose did Christ save you?

Verse 10 says, "We are his workmanship, created in Christ Jesus for good works, which God prepared beforehand, that we should walk in them."

Since God has already prepared good works for us, how should that affect how we spend our time and days?

In the Christian classic published in the 1930s, *Practicing His Presence,* author Frank Laubach decided that there was no reason he should not be able to dwell on Christ constantly. He disciplined his mind to surrender wholly to Christ on a moment-by-moment, conversation-by-conversation, activity-by-activity basis. After only a few weeks he journaled,

> I feel simply carried along each hour, doing my part in a plan which is far beyond myself. This sense of cooperation with God in little things is what so astonishes me, for I have never felt this way before. I need something, and turn round to find it waiting for me. I must work to be sure, but there is God working along with me. My part is to live this hour in continuous inner conversation with God and in perfect responsiveness to His will. This seems to be all I need to think about.

Is it possible we have complicated our lives until there is no room for Him and no space to hear the plans He has for us?

Two Feet

We are busy, and some things just have to get done . . . like laundry and dishes and dinner and diapers and so on. But what if we really looked to God for the things He wants us to set inside of our every day, inside of the mundane? The things He has for us to do here that will last forever? The things He planned for us before He made us? What would He say?

Where are the places God is calling you to make a mark in this life? It is short, after all.

What are the gifts that God has given you to use for His glory?

Who are your neighbors or coworkers who need God or time with you?

What are the causes that you are passionate about?

What are the unique opportunities God has laid in your path?

We do our best to live with one foot in heaven and one foot on earth, partaking in the everyday things of life and looking to participate in the things that last forever. It is a beautiful way to live.

God has an assignment for each one of us, and not because He wants us to have more to do. In fact, running around and doing every good thing is not what He wants from us. He is not pleased with random sacrificial service. He is pleased with obedience. It is better to obey than to sacrifice (1 Samuel 15:22).

He wants us to hear Him and obey.

With all the choices and decisions we have to make, to obey Him is simple . . . if we hear Him. It cuts down on options.

My sheep hear my voice, and I know them, and they follow me.

john 10:27

We are supposed to model our lives after Christ, and Jesus obeyed God. He listened to His Father and did whatever the Father said.

How do we hear the voice of God? The clearest way is through Scripture. We have to know and understand God and His truth before we can interpret any mysterious leading from His Spirit. But if we know truth and we are willing to follow God no matter what, we can pray for clarity and a clear feeling. God is rarely vague, though He is sometimes quiet.

God sent us the Holy Spirit to lead us, to help us. And we rarely depend on Him or let Him interact with our lives and schedules. We need to hear from Him if we are to accomplish the things He has for us here, the things He prepared in advance for us to carry out. We need to lean into Him.

I don't want to miss God's plans for me here.

As we begin to grasp the greater picture of God and His work around us, we long to become a part of the story. He wrote a part for each of us in this story—but most of us are ignoring Him and writing our own stories.

His story lasts forever, and the ones we write will melt away.

who are you, Lord? & what do you want from me?

Read 1 Peter 4:7–11. In light of what you read, answer the questions above.

imagine

No one can lay a foundation other than that which is laid, which is Jesus Christ. Now if anyone builds on the foundation with gold, silver, precious stones, wood, hay, straw—each one's work will become manifest, for the Day will disclose it, because it will be revealed by fire, and the fire will test what sort of work each one has done. If the work that anyone has built on the foundation survives, he will receive a reward. If anyone's work is burned up, he will suffer loss, though he himself will be saved, but only as through fire.

1 corinthians 3:11–15

Read 1 Corinthians 3:11-15. What do you believe separates the things that will burn up from the things that will last forever? (Look back at the passage in 1 Peter on page 101 that we just studied.)

Think about the day that you stand before God. If you know Christ, your eternity is secure, but Scripture on several occasions makes clear we will give an account for our gifts, money, and time. Write what you might say to God in that moment:

answer

Describe a time in your life that God was clearly leading you.

What did it feel like?

Was it easy to obey?

Did He seem real at that point? Did you doubt that it was God? What happened?

Do you routinely trust the Spirit of God in you to make decisions about your time and schedule?

For we are [God's] workmanship, created in Christ Jesus for good works, which God prepared beforehand, that we should walk in them.

ephesians 2:10

act

Draw a picture that represents your life right now:

Spend some time alone with the Lord, and pray about your schedule. What parts of your life and schedule are working and what things need to change?

consider

Strip away concerns about time, money, your abilities, your capacities, your life stage, your insecurities, and your reality. If all of these were not an issue, what would be the things God desires to do through you on this planet? Dream about this for a few minutes.

What are the things that come to mind?

_____

_____

_____

_____

_____

_____

_____

_____

When you stand before God at the end of your life, how will you feel if you don't do these things?

Control or God?

Sometimes we create our own chaos by saying yes to everything, and other times chaos is unavoidable, as in a season of raising young kids or when experiencing a tragedy. We want to stop the chaos by controlling our circumstances and trying to fix the feeling of being overwhelmed. There are some times that feeling overwhelmed by this life is inevitable—and in those moments God wants us to run to Him.

But you, O LORD, are a shield about me, my glory, and the lifter of my head.

psalm 3:3

Let Him shield you with His understanding of forever and His love for you.

In my life, the simple thought that God is the answer to all my problems seemed trite. It felt like making a wish to a genie in a bottle . . . praying, but nothing would come out.

All that while, He was there, beckoning me to find Him and to find freedom. But to do so I had to die. And honestly, I loved God, but I also loved me and I loved control—and I even loved my to-do lists and schedule. I wasn't sure I wanted God messing with everything. I wanted a little of Him, but not too much. But when we surrender, trust, and obey in the radical way He wants us to, as the old hymn says, the things of earth growing strangely dim in the light of His glory and grace.

Praise be to the God and Father of our Lord Jesus Christ, who has blessed us in the heavenly realms with every spiritual blessing in Christ. For he chose us in him before the creation of the world to be holy and blameless in his sight.

ephesians 1:3–4 NIV

God and forever—that is the story I want to join. That is the plan I want to be a part of.

He charted our course before the foundations of the earth. Our job is simply to live it out.

see ::

Watch video session six: OVERWHELMED

Use streaming instructions on inside cover or DVD.

Take notes if you like.

ask ::

Use session six: OVERWHELMED

Conversation Cards for group discussion.

sad :: 7

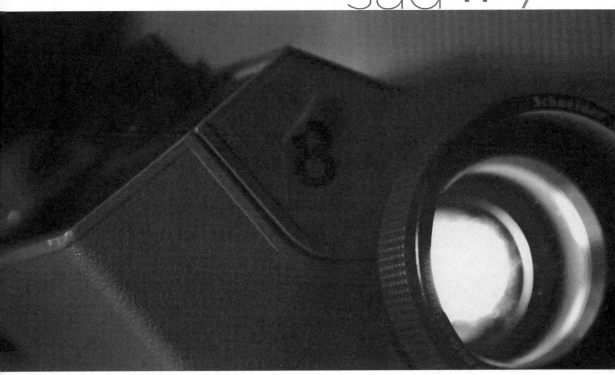

Work through pages 140–153 on your own before your next group
meeting and before you watch the next video teaching.

A Temporary Ache

As we approach this week on sadness, I know that we all come in with different experiences. No doubt some of you have lost a friend, spouse, parent, or child; some of you have walked through a decade-long battle with depression; or maybe you appear to be the happiest girl in the world, but inside you ache.

I just want to begin by saying, I am sorry.

We live in this screwed-up, broken mess of a place that deserves some cussing and crying sometimes.

Riley Jane is the eight-year-old daughter of one of my best friends. She is unable to eat, walk, talk, sing, or play. She has machines that help her breathe and a feeding tube. But Riley Jane can smile. Every time I see Riley, my first instinct is to feel sad. I walk up to her limp body with all these tubes running to and from her small frame.

But as soon as I see her face, I smile because this little light with the most beautiful eyes you have ever seen, smiles at me. (Now, I have to work a little for that smile! But she smiles.)

One day we were out at the lake together and I asked Riley, "Isn't it a beautiful day? Look at the sun," and she immediately looked up.

For the first time, I saw the real Riley Jane in there, understanding everything we say. A little eight-year-old girl in this broken mess of a body. She gets it—she gets how screwed up it all is, and yet she still smiles and looks for the sun. And my dear friend, Riley's mom, she smiles . . . a lot. She laughs and lives and smiles and loves.

I think they both know this is temporary. This is just a problem for a little while.

Problems are everywhere. People hurt us or leave us out. Our kids act out. Our job is demanding, or worse, boring. Our marriage is not easy. Or we find out we're sick with a cold, or sometimes it's cancer.

On even the best day, something still feels off inside. It is like a subtle, dull ache that never completely goes away. On bad days it is not subtle; it throbs. No one ever talks about it, but I think other people feel it. I think we all do.

For we know that the whole creation has been groaning together in the pains of childbirth until now. And not only the creation, but we ourselves, who have the firstfruits of the Spirit, groan inwardly as we wait eagerly for adoption as sons, the redemption of our bodies.

romans 8:22–23

---

study ::

read romans 8:18–39

Why are we sad?

Why is the world broken?

What is our hope?

We all know something is not right, and hear me, IT IS NOT RIGHT!

Yet we spend our thoughts, time, and money trying to make this life right, comfortable, safe, happy. Maybe we are spending all of this on the wrong things. Romans 8:25 says, "If we hope for what we do not yet have, we wait for it patiently" (NIV).

People, we are not patient. We who find it impossible to practice joy—is it because we can't see past today or this year or this life?

For this light momentary affliction is preparing for us an eternal weight of glory beyond all comparison, as we look not to the things that are seen but to the things that are unseen. For the things that are seen are transient, but the things that are unseen are eternal.

2 corinthians 4:18

My soul faints with longing for your salvation, but I have put my hope in your word.

psalm 119:81 NIV

Low Expectations

Hope is powerful—we are looking for it. Christians often assume that those who love God will be blessed financially and circumstantially, even physically . . . so we all start to hope in today and this world. But the Bible clearly tells us the world is cursed and fallen and broken and longing to be redeemed (Romans 8:19–20).

Romans 8:17 says, "Now if we are children, then we are heirs—heirs of God and co-heirs with Christ, if indeed we share in his sufferings in order that we may also share in his glory [future]" (NIV).

For to me to live is Christ [who suffered and died], and to die is [our] gain [our hope].

philippians 1:21

Our faith is built on invislble things that we hope in, not money and health, which are fleeting.

Those of us who love God are to be different from the world. We hope in bigger things than money or comfort or even health.

We live in such disappointment when our dreams are not fulfilled, as if God owes us something here and now. And oftentimes depression and discontentment rise out of our expectations for happy, fulfilling, short lives here on earth rather than the hope of eternity with our God in heaven.

For I consider that the sufferings of this present time are not worth comparing with the glory that is to be revealed to us.

romans 8:18

God wants us to hope, but He wants for us to hope in something way bigger than today. He desires for us to believe in Him and the place He is preparing for us, and to actually hope in it . . . wait for it . . . live for it.

But whatever gain I had, I counted as loss for the sake of Christ.

philippians 3:7

Denmark has been labeled as one of the happiest places to live on the planet. When researchers went in to try to discover why the people were so happy, they learned it was because they held relatively low expectations of their lives. As believers in God, we should be the same way. Not overly cynical but realistic. This life is just not meant to deliver. Our hope and expectations are for the next life, which will deliver beyond what we can dream.

The most cheerful people I have met, with few exceptions, have been those who've had the least sunshine and the most pain and suffering in their lives. The most grateful people I have ever known were not those who had traveled a pathway of roses all their lives, but those who were confined to their homes, some to their beds, and had learned to depend on God. The gripers, on the other hand, are usually those who have the least to complain about.

m. r. dehaan (1891–1965), former editor of *Our Daily Bread*

who are you, Lord? & what do you want from me?

Read 2 Corinthians 5:1–5, 7. In light of what you read, answer the questions above.

consider

The American Declaration of Independence says, "We hold these truths to be self-evident, that all men are created equal, that they are endowed by their Creator with certain unalienable Rights, that among these are Life, Liberty and the pursuit of Happiness."

Do you believe God wants us to strive after our own happiness?

Looking back at the verses we studied about suffering in Romans 8, where is a believer's hope found?

Write about your own pursuit of happiness and how that has impacted your walk with Christ:

_____

_____

_____

_____

_____

_____

question

What gets you down most consistently?

Are you avoiding something painful because it is too difficult?

When you are down, what do you turn to for comfort?

Look again at Romans 8:22–26. These verses suggest that believers in Christ are going to be sad / unsatisfied on this planet. How does that impact your views on depression and sadness in your own life?

Romans 8:26 says, "The Spirit himself intercedes for us with groanings too deep for words." What does that mean to you?

respond

Write a letter to God referring to Romans 8. Confess the things you have put your hope in besides God and your future home in heaven. If you feel that He is to blame for struggles in your life, be honest about that.

act

Get out of your comfort zone, and put yourself around people in need this week. While you are running errands or after work, stop by a homeless shelter, nursing home, soup kitchen, children's home—anywhere there are people truly in need. Maybe take one friend with you. Just talk to people and hear their stories. Find out what they need, feel, and believe. Afterward, answer the questions below.

How do they view their world?

What does hope look like for them?

How did time with them impact your own perspective on your life?

I tell you the truth, whatever you did for one of the least of these brothers of mine, you did for me.

matthew 25:40 NIV

Thankful

I love thankful people. I love kids who come over for a sleepover and go on and on because I made pancakes. I want to be like that. I believe gratitude is a direct result of expectations. Because we live in a time of plenty, even those of us who struggle financially are still so blessed we must consciously lower our expectations of people, of circumstances, of this planet. Let everything be human and flawed, and be completely taken and thankful when it is good. Allow people to surprise us more than they disappoint us.

It is so freeing to live gratefully, rather than live constantly disappointed. It is just more fun. And our gratefulness, our joy, comes from a pretty remarkable hope.

Therefore let us be grateful for receiving a kingdom that cannot be shaken.

hebrews 12:28

We are to be grateful and joyful people because we have such an immovable, fantastic hope. True joy is setting your heart on unmovable objects. There are only two unmovable objects that I know of . . . God and heaven.

see ::

Watch video session seven: SAD

Use streaming instructions on inside cover or DVD.

Take notes if you like.

ask ::

Use session seven: SAD

Conversation Cards for group discussion.

unstuck :: 8

Work through pages 160–173 on your own before your next group meeting and before you watch the next video teaching.

Sand Castles

If I am completely honest . . .

I felt stuck because I thought this life was supposed to make me happy, and I spent most of my time and energy building it. I needed my life to succeed. I needed to matter. I needed my kids to be happy. I needed everything to work out now. Letting go of this life freed me to receive whatever God has for me. We are going to see Him in just a little while, and that matters.

I felt stuck for so long because I did not believe God. I didn't believe in the gravity of my future and what my future cost. I did not believe that these minutes mattered so much, that they held so much purpose. I didn't believe God when He said that in order for me to live, I had to die. I felt stuck because I didn't understand God. I didn't understand what this relationship with Him meant, or what it meant to live dependent on His Spirit. I didn't understand how broken the world is—how broken I am. I didn't understand the bigger story and my part in it.

I felt stuck, most of all, because I was far from captivated by God's love for me. I thought He wanted my performance. I thought to know Him, to find joy and peace and God, I needed some secret formula. But He just wanted a relationship.

I could articulate the right stuff beautifully, but I was not living as if it were true. It did not punch me in the gut every morning. It did not get all of me. It did not move me to the point of change.

God seemed off in the distance somewhere, watching me build up my fancy, cute little life all around me, like a sand castle He knew would fall. But He patiently watched me build until I woke up and saw the sand—I saw the fragility of my work, the waste of it. Then He swept in with all that He is and all that He has for me. And I am done now with sand castles.

God is saying, *Die. Die to all you think you want, and trust Me.*

The overarching question of this study . . .

Are you willing to die? Because until our pride, our expectations, our plans, our desires, our will, our idols, and our very self dies . . . we are stuck.

study ::

read john 15:1–17

What is the fruit?

What is God's purpose for fruit?

What does God want to see in us and on this planet?

How do we participate in this?

Above all else, God wants us to need Him.

What are you leaving behind and what are you moving toward?

who are you, Lord? & what do you want from me?

Read Jeremiah 31:33–34. In light of what you read, answer the questions above.

A New Way

This new covenant . . . it is God in us. It is God through us. We no longer need a law controlling our behavior because God is able to freely move in, take over, and lead us down unique paths. The freedom that comes as we give God control is true freedom. But you have to know Him, not just hear about Him. These stuck places are the places we meet God. These dark places in our souls, if we let them, scream of our need for Him. And when I choose to go to the real living God . . .

He gives me forgiveness for my broken places.

He gives me grace for someone when I should be ticked off.

He gives me something bigger to want than temporary comfort.

He gives me peace when I am worried and spinning.

He gives me purpose for my days instead of feeling overwhelmed with my to-dos.

He gives me comfort and hope for a future, when life is falling apart.

But until you go to Him and see for yourself, He is simply a cliché. "Trust God" is either your source of life or a bumper sticker. If there is a God who made us, then He is everything, and He gets to say how to live. And our God is so clear about what He wants for us . . . what He wants for this life . . .

Whoever loves his life loses it, and whoever hates his life in this world will keep it for eternal life.

john 12:25

He is so patient to give us space to warm up to such a harsh statement. While we fight for our rights and wish for little things on this planet and worry about things that won't matter for long and grieve how broken things are around us . . . He waits. He waits for us to recognize the truth of His Word and the truth of what is ahead for those who know Him.

This life is fleeting. The next is not. He is not.

I pray that out of his glorious riches he may strengthen you with power through his Spirit in your inner being, so that Christ may dwell in your hearts through faith. And I pray that you, being rooted and established in love, may have power, together with all the saints, to grasp how wide and long and high and deep is the love of Christ, and to know this love that surpasses knowledge—that you may be filled to the measure of all the fullness of God.

ephesians 3:16–19 NIV

study

If we could just "grasp how wide and long and high and deep is the love of Christ," and "know this love that surpasses knowledge," then we would "be filled to the measure of all the fullness of God."

To be full of a God who never fades and knows everything and wins in the end and loves me . . . that would have to change everything. That would have to change me.

Before you head into the projects this week, reflect on the ways God has spoken to you in the past few weeks.

What has He shown you about Himself?

What has He shown you about yourself?

If there is one thing you walk away with from *Stuck*, I pray it is a bigger view of God. I pray that He has become more real to you. He wants us to see our need for Him. He wants us to depend on Him. Watch as He unfolds what it looks like to walk closely with Him as you work through these projects.

imagine

Draw a picture of what is happening in John 15:1–17: the vine, the fruit, the plan. This will help make sense of the roles we each play in relationship with God.

consider

Reading John 15:1–17, what does God want from you?

In the past, what has it felt like God has wanted from you?

Why do you think that God allows us to struggle, even though He is within us?

How sincerely do you act like you want a relationship with God? How intentional are you with Him?

No longer do I call you servants, for the servant does not know what his master is doing; but I have called you friends.

john 15:15

commit

This is it . . . Draw a line in the sand.

On the left, write what you are leaving behind. What has held you back from wholeheartedly allowing God to live through you for His purposes?

what I am leaving behind | what I am moving toward

On the right, write who you commit to be. What struggles are you yielding? What hopes will you pursue? What does it look like to live healthy in your mind, emotions, and relationships with God and others?

respond

Grab an hour with a friend or your spouse this week and share with him or her what God is teaching you about:

Himself

The state of your heart

His desires for you

Where to go from here

What it looks like for you to live experiencing freedom

As We Go from Here

I pray that everything is different, even if nothing has changed. Perspective is powerful. Knowing the God of the universe is world changing. I don't know what you came to this journey in hopes of finding, but I pray you leave with more of God.

Change is a process. Once we are saved, God begins the work of transformation. To do that work, He uses other people through the church; He uses His Word; He uses His Spirit; and He uses the stories and encouragement of others. I pray He has used all of those things these weeks and that you have journeyed further into freedom. He is completing the good work He has begun.

Our stuck places are the very places that make us ache for God. Even in our God-given limitations, He is gracious and tender. I need Him, and so I go to Him. He is there . . . God is there. God, who spins planets, is there waiting for me.

I love being with Him, and it is because I need Him that I go to Him. And something about just being near to Him unlocks my soul and I feel freer.

Are you unstuck? I pray you have tasted more freedom, but I pray that to be unstuck is not even your biggest goal anymore. I pray that you may know Christ and the power of His resurrection, "and to know the love of Christ that surpasses knowledge, that you may be filled with all the fullness of God" (Ephesians 3:19).

To know God and to be full to the brim with Him . . . may that become our biggest goal.

notes

see ::

Watch video session eight: UNSTUCK

Use streaming instructions on inside cover or DVD.

Take notes if you like.

ask ::

Use session eight: UNSTUCK

Conversation Cards for group discussion.

how to find god

Humanity had a perfect relationship with God until sin entered the world through Adam and Eve. With sin came the certainty of death and eternal separation from God. The penalty had to be paid. But at the same moment that He named the punishment for the first sin, God issued His promise to provide a way for us to return to Him.

Our sin was to be placed on the perfect sacrifice. God would send His own blameless, perfect Son to bear our sin and suffer our deserved fate—to get us back.

Jesus came, fulfilling thousands of years of prophecy, lived a perfect life, and died a gruesome death, satisfying the payment for our sin. Then after three days, He defeated death, rose from the grave, and is now seated with the Father.

Anyone who accepts the blood of Jesus for the forgiveness of their sin can be adopted as a child of God. To each one who believes, God issues His very own Spirit to seal and empower us to live this life for and with Him.

We were made for God, and He gave everything so that our souls could finally and forever find their rest in Him.

If you have never trusted Christ for the forgiveness of your sins, you can do that this moment. Just tell Him you need Him and tell Him you choose to trust Him as your Lord and Savior.

leader's guide

Leaders,

I am excited to partner with you in your efforts to pour into the lives of women! I pray that these few short pages will help to equip and prepare you to lead this study. Many of you may have led plenty of groups in the past, or perhaps this is the first you've led. Whichever the case, this is a spiritual calling and you are entering spiritual places with these women—and spiritual callings and places need spiritual power.

My husband, Zac, always says, "Changed lives change lives." If you are not first aware of your own need for life change, the women around you won't see their need. If you allow God into the inner struggles of your heart, the women following you will be much more likely to let Him into theirs. These women do not need to see bright and shiny, perfectly poised people; they need to see people who are a mess and daily dependent on God for their hope and strength.

Over and over again in Scripture we see God drawing near to the brokenhearted. On earth, Jesus moved toward sinners, saying things like, "Those who are well have no need of a physician, but those who are sick. I came not to call the righteous, but sinners" (Mark 2:17). So if you feel inadequate, as though you have no business leading a group of women, be encouraged; you are just the kind of person God wants to use!

I visited a halfway house once. All of the men were just out of prison. And with tears they confessed truly owning their weaknesses and mistakes. Their hearts were bleeding for the damage they had brought to those they love and gushing at how God had forgiven them.

I wanted to be like them—these men recovering from the consequences of sin. I wanted to need God like they did, feel broken like they were, and be transparent like they were. It was as if they were already exposed . . . already caught. "Screwed up" was written on their foreheads; they saw no need to act like it wasn't. And something about that brought freedom.

It's troubling to feel broken. It is troubling to need God. But we begin as leaders with humility as our posture. We begin with repentance because all of us have sin, even if it is invisible. Pray and confess the sin that you see within yourself, and ask God for His forgiveness. It will be easy for women to follow a humble leader who also needs God.

God wants to turn and heal us, but we must live sensitive to His Spirit and in awareness of our need for Him.

Together we can learn to let down our guards and go to God humbly. Together we can lead others in the same way. We can do this, together!

the vision

1. That we would see the broken spots in our souls as the very places God most wants to meet us. He longs for humanity to see our need for Him.

For my power is made perfect in weakness.

2 corinthians 12:9 NIV

---

2. That we would obey God. God longs to free us, but we have to obey Him. And He makes no small request of us. It is found in one word: *die*. He calls us to die. Die to our plans for our lives, our expectations, our pride, our rights. And in dying we find life.

   To know God and to be full to the brim with Him . . . may that become our biggest goal.

For we know that our old self was crucified with [Christ] so that the body of sin might be done away with, that we should no longer be slaves to sin—because anyone who has died has been freed from sin.

romans 6:6–7 NIV

---

3. That women would be pointed to God, a God worth dying for. The rest of this leader's guide is aimed at equipping you to point the women of your group to God in ways that will change their lives.

preparing yourself to lead a group

1. **Pray:** Pray like the world is ending, pray like this is the last chance for people to know Him, pray like our lives and futures depend on it, pray like the future of souls in heaven is at stake . . . Pray like you need God.

   Pray for your women:
   :: That God would show them the things holding them back and keeping them from freedom.
   :: That they would feel safe to open up and process.
   :: That they would want more of God and that God would meet them.
   :: That the conversation would be focused on God.
   :: That we would be humble displays of God's grace to these women.
   :: That God would come and fall on your time together.
   :: That many would come to a saving faith as they see God for who He is.

2. **Lean on God:** Allow the Holy Spirit to lead every moment together. We have provided you with tools that we will discuss in the next section; however, they are only tools to use as the Spirit leads you and your time together. God will have unique agendas for each of your groups as you depend on Him. Lean into your own weakness and into His strength and direction.

When Jesus left His disciples to go back to His Father in heaven, He said, "Don't go anywhere until you have the helper I will send you." We need to obey that same command. We don't begin until it is with the power of the Holy Spirit within us (see Acts 1:4–5). He is real and available and waiting to flood our lives and the lives around us as we serve and speak. But we have to wait for Him to speak, ask if we should speak and what we should speak, and ask what to do in different situations. God wants us to need Him and to depend on His Spirit. If this is not how you live on a daily basis, begin today.

3. **Be vulnerable:** If you choose not to be vulnerable, no one else will be. If you desire women to feel safe with you and your group, be vulnerable. This is not an optional assignment. This is your calling as you lead these women.

4. **Listen but also lead:** Listen as women share struggles. Some women are taking a tremendous risk in being vulnerable with you. Protect them by not interrupting and by instead empathizing. Do not feel the need to speak after each person shares. After most women have shared their answers to a question, turn it back to the scripture from the study guide, and help them process the truth and hope in their struggles. Avoid lecturing, but do bring the women back to truth.

5. **Model trust:** Be the example. Apply what you have learned and are learning through the study.

the study

Session Tools, How to Use Them, and Format

Stuck is designed to work in various types of venues and locations, including homes, dorm rooms, workplaces, or churches. Whether you find yourself leading a large group of people at church or a few neighbors in your home, the study is designed for small groups to share and process truth. I suggest a maximum number of eight in your group. If you are leading a large group at church, divide into smaller groups and enlist people to lead each small group.

Tools Needed

Study Guide. Each study guide comes with leader's guide and streaming video access. Every participant will need a Bible study guide. Distribute the books at your first group meeting, or have participants purchase and bring their guides on their own.

Conversation Card Deck. Group discussion questions and memory verse card for each session.

How To Use Your Tools

Each lesson is divided into three main sections:

Study

Point out the weekly Study section, followed by the Projects. These can be completed in one sitting or spaced throughout the week. The Study lessons in the book (except for the Introduction lesson) should be completed between group meetings.

The lessons are interactive, designed to help people study Scripture for themselves and apply it to their lives. The Projects in the Bible study guide provide creative options for applying Scripture. Some of these experiences may push participants outside their comfort zones. Encourage them to be brave and tackle the challenge. Make sure to discuss the Projects at each group meeting.

See

Watch the short, engaging video teaching to introduce the lesson via streaming or DVD to set the tone for your time together, and challenge your group to apply Scripture. If your group members want to take notes, encourage them to use the Notes page opposite each SEE title page. Each study guide includes instructions for personal access to streaming video on the inside front cover. This is perfect for anyone who might miss a group gathering, want to rewatch any of the video teaching, or if your group needs to meet on shortened time.

Ask

After the video teaching is complete, ask the group if anything in particular stood out while you prepare the Conversation Cards. The Conversation Cards provide a unique way to jump-start honest discussion. Each week's cards are labeled with the appropriate lesson title and can be used after the video or teaching time. The following is a suggested step-by-step way to use the cards.

:: Begin by laying out the Scripture Cards for that specific week.
:: Direct each group member to take a card.
:: Go over the Ground Rules each week. (Ground rules are found on page 12 and on the back of the Instruction card.)
:: Take turns presenting the question on each card to the group. Provide adequate time for everyone in your group to respond to each question.

Don't feel pressured to read and answer every card. Be sensitive to the leading of the Holy Spirit and your time constraints. Remind the group that what they share and how they share are entirely personal decisions. No one should be forced to answer every card.

NOTE:

Make use of this leader's guide to facilitate a great Bible study experience for your group. It will help you point people to the overarching theme for each lesson and will give you specific suggestions on how to share the truth and foster discussion.

Session Format

This eight-session study is designed to go deep very quickly, so it's flexible when considering the length of your group sessions. It can be led in a church spread out over a couple of hours, or in a break room over a one-hour lunch. However, the more time you can allow for discussion, the better. When the group is given deep questions and space to reflect and respond, you'll be surprised by the depth and beauty of the conversations.

You will be the best judge of what time and format works for your group. However, here is a suggested schedule for each group meeting.

1. **OPEN—Personal study discussion** (15–35 minutes)

   After a warm welcome and opening prayer, provide time for the group to share and discuss their personal reflections from the Study of Scripture and the Projects. If you have more than eight in your group, break into smaller groups for this discussion.

2. **SEE—Video teaching** (7–8 minutes)

   Use the video to lay the foundation for the week's lesson and transition to the Conversation Cards. Feel free to provide supplemental teaching for your group.

3. **ASK—Conversation Cards** (25–75 minutes)

   Allow time for each group member to ask and discuss the question on each card. If you need an extra set of cards, they are available for purchase from your favorite online retailer.

4. CLOSE—Closing (5–10 minutes)

Pray as a group and encourage everyone to engage in the Study before meeting again.

Tips For Leading Your Group

Always encourage the group members to abide by the following Ground Rules for discussion. These rules can be found below, on the back of the Instruction Card, and on page 12 of this Bible study book.

Be Concise

Share your answer to the questions while protecting others' time for sharing. Be considerate. Don't be afraid to share with the group but try not to dominate the conversation.

Keep Group Members' Stories Confidential

Your group members will want to share sensitive and personal information with you, not with your husband or other friends. Protect each other by not allowing anything shared in the group to leave the group.

Rely On Scripture For Truth

Conventional, worldly wisdom has value, but it is not absolute truth. Only Scripture provides that. In your times of discussion, be careful not to equate good advice with God's truth.

No counseling

Work together to protect the group by not directing all attention toward solving one person's problem. This is the place for confessing and discovery and applying truth together as a group. However, at times a member may need to dig even deeper with an outside counselor or talk with a friend outside of small group time. If that is you, don't be afraid to ask for help, or be sure and follow up with a member of the group.

When To Refer

Some of the people in your group may be dealing with issues beyond your ability to help. If you sense that someone may need more extensive help, refer them to speak with your pastor or a trained Christian counselor. Maintain the relationship and follow up with them to make sure they are getting the care needed. You or someone else in your group may need to walk with them through this season of their life. As we have said many times, be sensitive to the Holy Spirit's leading as you love and offer hope to the people in your group.

Types Of Learners

Hopefully, you will be blessed to be leading this study with a group diverse in age, experience, and style. While the benefits of coming together as a diverse group to discuss God outweigh the challenges by a mile, there are often distinctions in learning styles. Just be aware and consider some of the differences in different types of learning styles that may be represented. (These are obviously generalizations, and each person as an individual will express their own unique communication style, but in general these are common characteristics.)

Experiential Learners

There are women who are more transparent, don't like anything cheesy, want to go deep quickly, and are passionate. Make a safe environment for them by being transparent yourself and engaging their hearts. These women may not care as much about head knowledge and may care more deeply how knowledge about God applies to their lives. They want to avoid being put in a box. Keep the focus on applying truth to their lives and they will stay engaged. Don't preach to them; be real and show them through your experiences how to pursue the mind of Christ.

Pragmatic Learners

These women are more accustomed to a traditional, inductive, or precept approach to Bible study. They have a high value for truth and authority but may not place as high a value on the emotional aspects of confessing sin and being vulnerable. To them it may feel unnecessary or dramatic. Keep the focus on the truth of Scripture.

These women keep truth in the forefront of their lives and play a valuable role in discipleship.

Because this study is different from traditional studies, some women may need more time to get used to the approach of this study. The goal is still to make God big in our lives, to fix our minds on Him, and to choose where to train our thoughts. We all just approach it in unique ways to reach unique types of people. I actually wrote this study praying it could reach both types of learners. I am one who lives with a foot in both worlds, trying to apply the deep truths I gained in seminary in an experiential way. I pray that this study would deeply engage the heart and the mind, and that we would be people who worship God in spirit and in truth, not just learning about the battle for our minds but going to war for them together.

Common struggles like fear, stress, anger, shame, and insecurity are not respecters of age, religion, or income level. These struggles are human, and I have seen this study transcend the typical boundaries of Christian and seeker, young and old, single and married, needy and comfortable, bringing these women together and to God in a unique and powerful way.

In the following pages and notes for each *Stuck* lesson, I hope I have given you enough guidance that you do not feel lost, but enough freedom to depend on the Holy Spirit. These are only suggestions, but hopefully these notes will help surface themes and goals to guide you through your discussion of group members' homework and through the discussion of the Ask conversation cards. The video, homework, and cards should provide more than enough material for great discussions, but stay on track, and be sure people are walking away with hope and truth.

introduction :: 1

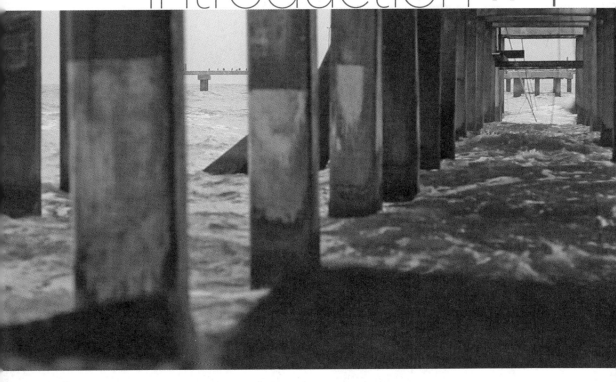

Note to leader: The teaching format for this session is different than the other sessions because it is the first group time and there is no personal study to review. Participants are encouraged to complete the Introduction material on pages 15-20 on their own to acclimate to the purpose of this study. These pages can be done after viewing and discussing the video or on their own time.

OPEN

Welcome the participants to your group and take a few moments for introductions. Briefly share about yourself and allow others to do the same. After introductions, lead the group in prayer.

Distribute the Bible study guides to group members and go over the Instructions and Expectations on page 10. Explain and show them their individual access to streaming video so everyone can keep up with the study, regardless of an unavoidable missed gathering.

SEE

View video session one: INTRODUCTION: STUCK

ASK

Transition to the Conversation Cards for discussion. The cards for this week are labeled "STUCK" on the front. Lead participants to choose, answer, and discuss the questions on the cards. (You can review the instructions for using the cards in ASK on page 186.)

CLOSE

Close by asking the group to write down three things:

:: one thing they learned from this session;

:: one reason they are excited about this study;

:: one question they have moving forward.

Briefly discuss their responses. Do so with little or no commentary but paying close attention to the answers. If time allows, close by praying specifically for each person in your group, using one of each person's responses as the focus of your prayer for them.

He who conceals his sins does not prosper, but whoever confesses and renounces them finds mercy.

proverbs 28:13 NIV

Instruct the group to complete Session 2: BROKEN Study and Projects before the next group meeting.

broken :: 2

MAIN IDEA: This week we are studying the struggle between the Spirit and our flesh that has been warring since before God spun planets. We define this universal problem as the Spirit of life and peace versus the law of sin and death (Romans 8). We must begin here with the problem.

Here are some general goals for your time together this week:
:: Identify and define the war we all feel and see around us.
:: Help the women see their need for God, because of their sin.
:: Help the women come out of hiding behind pride or shame and confess the places of sin or hurt in their souls.
:: See God's plan and hope for sin and weakness in our lives.
:: Prepare to begin this journey humbly united in need of God.

1. OPEN

Suggestions on places to focus as you go over the homework with your group:
:: Ask the group to share specifically about the war they studied in Romans 8.
:: Ask what they think God's goal is in allowing our weaknesses and neediness.
:: Discuss their response to Project 4.
:: Ask what else they learned as they studied and interacted with the lesson and Scripture this week.

2. SEE

Watch video session two: BROKEN.

3. ASK

Transition to the Conversation Cards to continue your discussion. The cards for this week are labeled "BROKEN" on the front. Lead the group to choose, answer, and discuss the questions on the cards. (You can review the instructions for using the cards in ASK on page 186).

4. CLOSE

Read this week's Scripture memory verse aloud to the group and instruct the group to commit each verse to memory each week as best they can.

"My grace is sufficient for you, for my power is made perfect in weakness." Therefore I will boast all the more gladly about my weaknesses, so that Christ's power may rest on me. That is why, for Christ's sake, I delight in weaknesses, in insults, in hardships, in persecutions, in difficulties. For when I am weak, then I am strong.

2 corinthians 12:9–10 NIV

Encourage the group to complete Session 3: MAD Study and Projects before the next group meeting.

mad :: 3

MAIN IDEA: Anger is my reaction when my rights are being taken from me. We all live with basic assumptions about these rights. But Jesus calls us to a surrender that is so resolute, so final, that to lift our head in protest about our rights would seem insane. He laid down His rights in heaven and laid down His very life, being misunderstood by the world to the point of being brutally killed. And somehow, even though it feels like death, in laying down my rights, I find freedom.

NOTE: Take careful note to not imply that we are to endure abuse. You may have group members who have been physically, sexually, or otherwise abused in their pasts, or are being abused now. At the beginning of your time with the group, stress that God does not expect us to endure abuse, and offer to stay after the meeting to talk with anyone who needs help.

Here are some general goals for your time together this week:

:: Focus on the truth that the hidden rights we claim are often the source of anger and resentment when we feel threatened.

:: Point to the fact that Scripture calls us to lay down our rights over and over again.

:: Help the women see that in laying down our rights, we respond in a way that demonstrates God to our world.

:: Emphasize that in laying down our rights we find freedom from bitterness and resentment.

:: Remember that God is worth the abandonment of our rights.

1. OPEN

Begin by reviewing the personal study from last week. Here are some suggested places to focus as you review:

:: How did the verses in James impact your view of anger?

:: What are some of the rights that you feel entitled to?

:: Look at the passage in Luke on page 43 in the study guide. How does this impact your view of our rights?

:: How did you feel in your home as a child in the presence of anger? Discuss Project 3.

2. SEE

Watch video session three: MAD

3. ASK

Transition to the Conversation Cards to continue your discussion. The cards for this week are labeled "MAD" on the front. Lead the group to choose, answer, and discuss the questions on the cards. (You can review the instructions for using the cards in ASK on page 186.). Remember to begin with the Scripture card and end by stressing the scriptural truth group members can apply to their lives as a result of what they discussed in your group time. Close this discussion by praying for the things shared and praising God for His position in our lives and in eternity.

4. CLOSE

Read this week's Scripture memory verse aloud to the group and instruct the group to commit each verse to memory each week as best they can.

If anyone would come after me, let him deny himself and take up his cross and follow me. For whoever would save his life will lose it, but whoever loses his life for my sake will find it. For what will it profit a man if he gains the whole world and forfeits his soul? Or what shall a man give in return for his soul?

matthew 16:24–26

Close with prayer.

Encourage the group to complete Session 4: DISCONTENT Study and Projects before the next group meeting.

discontent :: 4

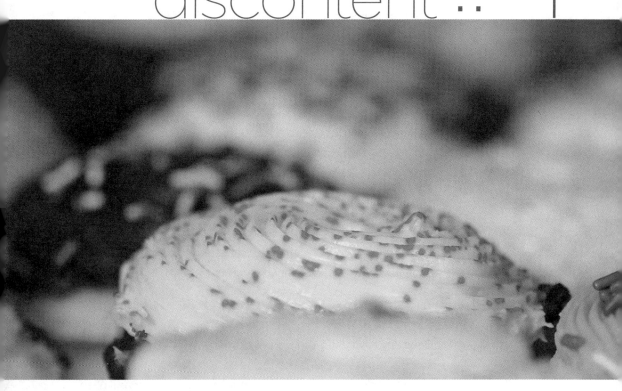

MAIN IDEA: Discontentment is plaguing the souls of women. Big things and small things—we want something more, something different. And our souls are sick about it. We are chasing wind. All the while, there is a giant story in the background that we can barely make out because we are so distracted. We are missing the point above it all . . . we are missing God, who wants to fill our discontented souls.

Here are some general goals for your time together this week:

:: Define the areas in which women are struggling with discontentment. These could be materialism, body image, and so on.

:: Come to an understanding that discontentment is sin and it is making us distracted and numb to God's bigger purposes. We are chasing the wind.

:: Help the women see that freedom from discontentment is found in delayed gratification—hoping for heaven.

We all long to be known and loved, and this desire often drives us to search in the wrong places. God created us with the desire to be known and loved, and only He can truly fill that desire.

1. OPEN

Begin by reviewing the personal study from last week. Here are some suggested places to focus as you review:

:: What did you learn as you worked through Romans 12 and John 12?

:: What was your response to Katie's blog in Project 1?

:: Discuss your lists in Project 4.

2. SEE

Watch video session four: DISCONTENT

3. ASK

Transition to the Conversation Cards to continue your discussion. The cards for this week are labeled "DISCONTENT" on the front. Lead the group to choose, answer, and discuss the questions on the cards. (You can review the instructions for using the cards in ASK on page 186.) Remember to begin with the Scripture card and end by stressing the scriptural truth group members can apply to their lives as a result of what they discussed in your group time. Close this discussion by praying for the things shared and praising God for His position in our lives and in eternity.

4. CLOSE

Read this week's Scripture memory verse aloud to the group and instruct the group to commit each verse to memory each week as best they can.

Whoever loves his life loses it, and whoever hates his life in this world will keep it for eternal life. If anyone serves me, he must follow me; and where I am, there will my servant be also. If anyone serves me, the Father will honor him.

john 12:25–26

Close with prayer.

Encourage the group to complete Session 5: SCARED Study and Projects before the next group meeting.

MAIN IDEA: We worry about what we value. With no God, we value only what we see. We value today because it is all we have. But if that other kingdom is real and does last forever . . . something must change. We have to face what we fear. The bigger God gets, the less we live in fear.

Here are some general goals for your time together this week:
:: Develop an understanding that we worry about what we value and it often becomes an idol above God (e.g., people's approval, our children's behavior, our health, hobbies, money).
:: Help the women see that trust is the most obvious indicator that we truly believe in God. If we do not trust Him, we have to ask if we believe He loves us and that He is sovereign.
:: Challenge each other to die to your hopes for this life and receive whatever God has for you, even if it is difficult or costly.
:: Embrace the truth that we have to kill our idols and trust our God.

1. OPEN

Begin by reviewing the personal study from last week. Here are some suggested places to focus as you review:
:: What did you learn about God and His love and care for you in Matthew 6?
:: What did you think of Isaiah 2? Do you see any idols in your life?
:: What amount of your thought life is tied up in worry or fear? Discuss Project 1.
:: Talk about what was in the blank at the bottom of Project 4.

2. SEE

Watch video session five: SCARED

3. ASK

Transition to the Conversation Cards to continue your discussion. The cards for this week are labeled "SCARED" on the front. Lead the group to choose, answer, and discuss the questions on the cards. (You can review the instructions for using the cards in ASK on page 186.) Remember to begin with the Scripture card and end by stressing the scriptural truth group members can apply to their lives as a result of what they discussed in your group time. Close this discussion by praying for the things shared and praising God for His position in our lives and in eternity.

4. CLOSE

Read this week's Scripture memory verse aloud to the group and instruct the group to commit each verse to memory each week as best they can.

The LORD is my shepherd. . . . Even though I walk through the valley of the shadow of death, I will fear no evil, for you are with me; your rod and your staff, they comfort me. . . . Surely goodness and mercy shall follow me all the days of my life, and I shall dwell in the house of the LORD forever.

psalm 23:1, 4, 6

Close with prayer.

Encourage the group to complete Session 6: OVERWHELMED Study and Projects before the next group meeting.

overwhelmed :: 6

MAIN IDEA: For many of us, busyness is our drug of choice. It makes us numb. We stay busy so that we don't have to think about anything too messy, too difficult. We don't want to feel our stuck places. Rather than depend on the Spirit to carry us along in our predestined journey, we allow the rope of our insignificant schedules to drag us under the boat—drowning us.

God charted our courses even before He created the foundations of the earth—our job is simply to live them out.

Here are some general goals for your time together this week:

:: Know that God prepared good deeds for us to carry out before time began (Ephesians 2:10).

:: Ask each other: Are you depending on the Holy Spirit to lead your minutes and days, or are you dependent on yourself?

:: See that God leading and empowering our actions is what separates the things that will last from the wasted things (1 Corinthians 3:11–15).

:: Know that God doesn't want us to do important, showy things; He wants us to simply obey Him (His Spirit inside of us and His word through Scripture) on a moment-by-moment basis.

:: The expectation throughout Scripture is that we would radically reorient our lives around the gospel and God's agenda upon our salvation. Ask each other: Have you rearranged your time and life?

NOTE: Before leaving this week, take a look at Project 4 in the next lesson SAD on page 151 of the study guide. Schedule that time together for this coming week.

1. OPEN

Begin by reviewing the personal study from last week. Here are some suggest

:: What did you learn about God in Ephesians 2?

:: What are we to do according to 1 Peter 4? Why are we to do it?

:: Talk about Project 1 and the valuable things we are doing and the things that are wasted.

:: Dream together over Project 4.

2. SEE

Watch video session six: OVERWHELMED

3. ASK

Transition to the Conversation Cards to continue your discussion. The cards for this week are labeled "OVERWHLEMED" on the front. Lead the group to choose, answer, and discuss the questions on the cards. (You can review the instructions for using the cards in ASK on page 186.) Remember to begin with the Scripture card and end by stressing the scriptural truth group members can apply to their lives as a result of what they discussed in your group time. Close this discussion by praying for the things shared and praising God for His position in our lives and in eternity.

4. CLOSE

Read this week's Scripture memory verse aloud to the group and instruct the group to commit each verse to memory each week as best they can.

For we are [God's] workmanship, created in Christ Jesus for good works, which God prepared beforehand, that we should walk in them.

ephesians 2:10

Close with prayer.

Encourage the group to complete Session 7: SAD Study and Projects before the next group meeting.

sad :: 7

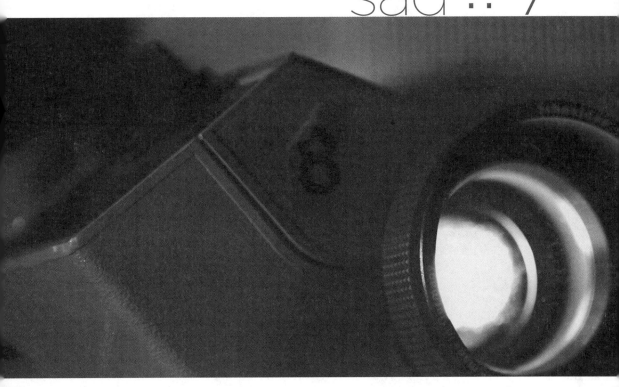

MAIN IDEA: We all know something is not right; and hear me, it is not right! Yet, we spend our thoughts, time, and money trying to make life right, comfortable, safe, happy. Maybe we are spending all of this energy on the wrong things. Romans 8:25 says, "If we hope for what we do not yet have, we wait for it patiently" (NIV).

Here are some general goals for your time together this week:
:: Understand that until Christ returns, sadness is a part of our lives and this planet.
:: Help the women to see that if our goal is happiness, we will never arrive at our goal and will never be able to grow up and obey God.
:: Remember that sadness points to our longing for heaven and for God. Draw near to Him in it.
:: Clearly define and talk about a believer's hope and how we can live hopeful today.

1. OPEN

Begin by reviewing the personal study from last week. Here are some suggested places to focus as you review:
:: What did you learn in Romans 8?
:: Why is sadness okay? And what is our hope?
:: Talk about Projects 1 and 4.

2. SEE

Watch video session seven: SAD

3. ASK

Transition to the Conversation Cards to continue your discussion.
The cards for this week are labeled "SAD" on the front. Lead the
group to choose, answer, and discuss the questions on the cards.
(You can review the instructions for using the cards in ASK on
page 186.) Remember to begin with the Scripture card and end by
stressing the scriptural truth group members can apply to their lives
as a result of what they discussed in your group time. Close this
discussion by praying for the things shared and praising God for His
position in our lives and in eternity.

4. CLOSE

Read this week's Scripture memory verse aloud to the group and
instruct the group to commit each verse to memory each week as
best they can.

*We look not to the things that are seen but to the things that are unseen. For the things that are seen
are transient, but the things that are unseen are eternal.*

2 corinthians 4:18

Close with prayer.

Encourage the group to complete Session 8: UNSTUCK Study and
Projects before the next group meeting.

unstuck :: 8

MAIN IDEA: Use this session as a chance to really hear from your women about how they have grown and what they need in order to move forward. Celebrate, pray, and challenge them as you conclude this journey together. Our stuck places are the very places that make us ache for God. These don't completely go away until heaven. But knowing more of God changes everything and begins to fill us.

Here are some general goals for your time together this week:
:: Understand that our freedom is found in dying to ourselves and trusting God.
:: Know that our hope is heaven, and anything less will disappoint.
:: Challenge each other to live out our mission, which is to obey God and live displaying the gospel.
:: Challenge each other to see that life is short; we should probably get after it, since we know how this all ends!

1. OPEN

Begin by reviewing the personal study from last week. Here are some suggested places to focus as you review:
:: Look at John 15, and talk about the power of a relationship with God.
:: What changed in the new covenant in Jeremiah 31?
:: Look at the drawings in Project 1.
:: Spend time on Project 3. Have everyone share their answer to the question: What are you leaving behind and what are you moving toward? (This is one of the Ask cards for this week.)

2. SEE

Watch video session eight: UNSTUCK

3. ASK

Transition to the Conversation Cards to continue your discussion. The cards for this week are labeled "UNSTUCK" on the front. Lead the group to choose, answer, and discuss the questions on the cards. (You can review the instructions for using the cards in ASK on page 186.) Remember to begin with the Scripture card and end by stressing the scriptural truth group members can apply to their lives as a result of what they discussed in your group time. Close this discussion by praying for the things shared and praising God for His position in our lives and in eternity.

4. CLOSE

Share your personal experience you've had in these weeks together. Allow the group to share similar stories. If a member of your group is having difficulty with this idea or facing anxiety about it, take a moment to surround them and pray for them.

Read this week's Scripture memory verse aloud to the group and remind the group to go back through all the memory verses from weeks two through seven. Encourage them to keep committing these verses to memory as they continue through the process of growing out of being stuck and into freedom—these verses will guide them and lead them well.

sources

Majors, Katie. Kisses from Katie blog, November 29, 2001, https://katiemajors.blog/about.

DeHaan, M. R. *Broken Things*. Grand Rapids, MI: Zondervan, 1967, 43–44.

Elliot, Elisabeth. *Keep a Quiet Heart*. Ann Arbor, MI: Servant, 1995, 18–19; emphasis in original.

Keller, Tim. "Talking About Idolatry in a Postmodern Age." Monergism.com, April 2007. http://www.monergism.com/postmodernidols.html.

Lawrence, Brother and Frank Laubach. *Practicing His Presence*. Jacksonville, FL: SeedSowers Christian Books Publishing, orig. 1973, repr. 1988, 5. Journal entry dated January 29, 1930.

Lewis, C. S. *The Weight of Glory*. New York: HarperOne, orig. 1949, repr. 2001, 26.

Meyer, Rev. F. B in *Streams in the Desert*. L. B. Cowman, comp. Grand Rapids, MI: Zondervan, orig. 1925, repr. 1996, January 14; emphasis in original.

Murray, Andrew. *Humility: The Journey Toward Holiness*. Grand Rapids, MI: Bethany House, orig. 1896, repr. 2001, 73.

Nouwen, Henri. J. M. *The Road to Daybreak: A Spiritual Journey*. New York: Image, orig. 1988, repr. 1990, 183–84.

Tozer, A. W. *The Knowledge of the Holy*. New York: HarperOne, orig. 1961, repr. 1978, 1.

Tozer, A.W. *The Pursuit of God*. Camp Hill, PA: WingSpread, orig. 1957, repr. 1992, 97; paraphrased.

Also Available from Jennie Allen

Building Deep Community in a Lonely World

This seven-session video Bible study looks at the original community in Genesis and the Trinity to see how God intended for us to live in community all along.

Identify the Threads of Your Life

In this eight-session video Bible study using the story of Joseph, Jennie explains how his suffering, gifts, story, and relationships fit into the greater story of God—and how your story can do the same.

Stopping the Spiral of Toxic Thoughts

In this six-session, video Bible study, Jennie inspires and equips us to transform our emotions, our outlook, and even our circumstances by taking control of our thoughts.

What the Bible Tells Us About Our Emotions

This six-session video Bible study teaches how your emotions actually help you notice what's wrong and connect with God and others more deeply.

You are Enough Because Jesus is Enough.

In this eight-session video Bible study, Jennie Allen walks through key passages in the Gospel of John that demonstrate how Jesus is enough. We don't have to prove anything because Jesus has proven everything.

Chasing After the Heart of God

Chase is an eight-session video Bible study experience to discover the heart of God and what it is exactly He wants from us through major events in the life of David and the Psalms.

Visit JennieAllen.com for more info. Available wherever books & Bibles are sold.